THE CARPENTERS' COMPANY 1786 RULE BOOK

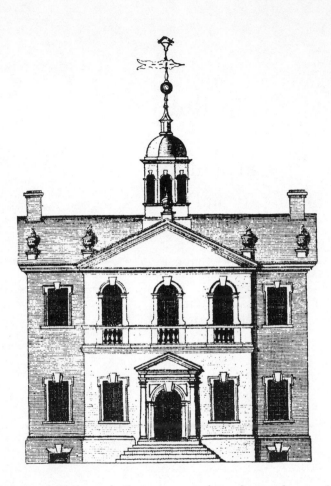

Carpenters' Hall was built in 1770–73 from designs by member Robert Smith.

North or front elevation. Except for the entrance (completed in 1792 according to a somewhat different design), the urns on the roof (apparently never installed), and the weathervane (note dividers-and-compass finial), the building has come through the years with little change.

In this building the First Continental Congress met in the Fall of 1774.

The Rules of Work

of the

Carpenters' Company

of the City and County of Philadelphia

1786

with the original copper plate illustrations

annotated, with an Introduction, by
Charles E. Peterson, F.A.I.A.

BELL PUBLISHING COMPANY

Acknowledgments: To Professor Louise Hall of Duke University
for data traded many years ago; to architect Orville W. Carroll of
Rome, New York, for the loan of electrostatic copies of other price
books; to architect Lee H. Nelson of the National Park Service at
Philadelphia, for good suggestions; and to Thomas S. Keefer, Jr.,
of the CCCCP, for many years of encouragement.

CHARLES E. PETERSON

Members of this Company
who designed and built so well
the colonial metropolis of Philadelphia,
who offered our Hall for the dangerous adventure
of the first Continental Congress,
who restored it as a Revolutionary landmark in 1857
and have cared for it ever since,
we remember you with respect and gratitude.

CONTENTS

*explanatory notes accompany each plate

INTRODUCTION

NEARLY TWENTY YEARS AGO the present writer, rummaging through the attic of Carpenters' Hall, came across an old wooden packing box containing some copies of the Company's 1786 price book titled *Articles and Rules.* Because it is almost unknown and yet of potential value to modern historians, it is being published again.[1]

There is no mystery about its scarcity: the little volume had been in its own time highly restricted as a trade secret. Any member showing it to outsiders was liable to expulsion and when he died, the Company promptly called on the widow for his copy. Even Thomas Jefferson, writing from Charlottesville, was unable to obtain one as late as 1817.[2] It is hoped that this rare work will be of interest to students of the American building industry for which early literature of any kind is uncommon. As far as is known, it is the first illustrated price book exclusively about carpentry.

Architectural historians may well ask the question: is this the first illustrated American work on architecture? The answer is not simple. The first books on that subject published here were Abraham Swan, *The British Architect* and *A Collection of Designs in Architecture,* both produced in Philadelphia by the architect-engraver John Norman in 1775.[3] But these were only new editions of works published earlier in London.[4]

The price book devoted *solely* to carpenters' work seems to be a peculiarly American institution and the present illustrated book is apparently unique for the eighteenth century. Building practices in the English colonies were naturally derived from those in the mother country, but the subject of pricebooks there does not seem to have been investigated and written upon in any definitive way.[5] The Royal Institute of British Architects' great library in London has the best collection of early technical books. Research there this past summer seems to indicate that the RIBA library has only one price book exclusively devoted to carpentry: Isaac Harrison, Robert Jackson, Matthew Nelson and William Potts, *The Carpenters' and Joiners' Price Book* (Liverpool, 1811).[6] All of this reflects the fact that carpentry was not the dominant trade in England where wood frame buildings were no longer being built in the cities.

The first design book especially aimed at the New World builder may well have been that of M. D'Albaret, an architect of Paris, titled *Differns Projets Relatifs au Climat et à la Manière la plus Convenable de Bâtir dans les Pays Chauds et plus Particulierement dans les Indes Occidentales* and issued in 1776. It is essentially a portfolio of twenty large engravings illustrating nine ambitious house projects designed by the author. D'Albaret believed that "a book setting out a method of building adapted to the local conditions would be welcomed by people at present living in the West Indies and by those who intend to settle there." It seems unlikely that this pretentious collection of designs ever had much influence in the French West Indies where (apparently unknown to M. D'Albaret) an indigenous style had developed, one that was suitable to the Caribbean with its own special problems.[7]

Books published especially for the use of the American building mechanic were slow in coming. Only as the technology of building became more varied and complicated in the nineteenth century were they provided in any numbers. The Philadelphia *Articles and Rules* book was a strictly American production illustrated with drawings made by Company member Thomas Nevell[8] of structural and decorative elements used in Philadelphia. Although modest in format alongside the great folio volumes of London and the continent, it can be called the first really American work. It is more than a price book. The fact that it was illustrated by copper plates delineating both the classical orders and designs for such elements of buildings as chimney-pieces, fanlights, dormer windows and fancy railings (in this case, Chinese) entitles it to be considered in part as a "pattern book." The plates were probably shown to prospective owners (or their wives) who were thereby induced to put up something more ambitious architecturally than the plain Quaker work that had theretofore predominated. These sober-minded gentlemen may have looked at earlier English works such as William Salmon, Jr.'s *Palladio Londinensis: of the London Art of Building* (London, 1734), which contained some illustrations of doors and windows, and a very small section on the pricing of carpenters' work. The work was evidently popular in England for it was already in its sixth edition by 1762; a copy of the 1752 edition was available in Philadelphia.[9] In no way, however, could it have served the purpose intended by Philadelphia's own *Articles and Rules* book.

Over the centuries several different categories of architectural works had been produced. First of all came the books of the Renaissance. The earliest were written in Latin, published in Italy, and printed by Germans in small issues.[10] An obscure London paperstainer named John Shute who had, under the patronage of the Duke of Northumberland, visited Italy to confer with the masters, produced the first in the English language. It was dedicated to Queen Elizabeth, illustrated by some copper plates of "the orders" extravagantly executed, and issued in 1563. In addressing the reader it takes a very high tone, indeed. One can picture milord, fortified by Shute's report on the architecture of ancient Rome, rushing out of his study to argue with the old boss builder struggling to finish the new wing. But through such works as Shute's the Renaissance became an early and permanent industry in England and elsewhere; the book trade is still busy with it.

Down through the years books on Architecture (with a capital A) multiplied. The perennial publishers' darling was Vitruvius, an obscure Roman architect whose essays on design and construction had managed to survive the Middle Ages in manuscript form. His famous aphorism concerning "Firmness, Commodity and Delight" has been serviceable to all generations of writers, especially after illustrations were (for the first time) supplied by Renaissance draftsmen. Even Vitruvius' advice on masonry construction, as irrelevant to modern practices as Julius Caesar's puzzling description of his bridge over the Rhine, has been solemnly and repeatedly translated and annotated by scholars everywhere.

Except for the classical orders used in high-style buildings—and which were early pressed and frozen by Sebastiano Serlio and Giacomo Barozzi da Vignola into their personal molds of "correctness"—these books had little to offer the practical builder who was not a literary person, though presumably, just as intelligent as anyone else.[11] Sir Henry Wotten's engaging little volume called *The Elements of Architecture* (1624) lamented the fact (and this is too often true today) that those who had the technical knowledge lacked "Gramer" and that those who were getting out books were short on knowledge. He was, however, heartened to believe that Leon Battista Alberti, "the first learned Architect beyond the Alps," had been qualified in both fields, though already dead for a century and a half.[12]

Right after the Great Fire of London appeared Stephen Primatt's small volume titled *The City and Country Purchaser and Builder* (1667) offering much practical advice to the owner of city lots and the building entrepreneur. In it the business of "mensuration," or measuring, is discussed along with the trades of the carpenter, bricklayer, plasterer, joiner, painter, glazier, and mason. Primatt offered only two floor plans and one street elevation for a city house and one design for a panelled chimney frontispiece (as does, incidentally, the little book being introduced here).

In London a decade after Primatt appeared Joseph Moxon's *Mechanicks Exercises, or the Doctrine of Handy-Works,* a work of very different character.[13] In apologizing for writing about such a lowly subject its author admits that, while one might brush up against some sordid or ignoble characters among the house carpenters,

> it is very well known that many Gentlemen in the Nation of good Rank and high Quality are conversant in Handy-Works [read hobby shops] . . . . How pleasant and healthy this their Diversion is, their Minds and bodies find; and how harmless and honest all sober men may judge.[14]

These genteel hobbyists were clearly the parties expected to buy the book. It is hard to imagine an apprentice to the trade, in London under guild supervision by the Worshipful Company of Carpenters (chartered in the fourteenth century),[15] learning his craft from a book. Moxon's text, though, contains a great deal of practical advice made from close observation and the tools mentioned are well illustrated. He does not go into the matter of mensuration.

The French books, incidentally, did not neglect technology. Philibert de L'Orme (c. 1515–1570), the leading French theorist of the Renaissance, brought out a volume of roof framing details in 1561 copiously illustrated with woodcuts and entitled *Nouvelles Inventions pour bien bastir* even before his first book on design. Another French writer, Mathurin Jousse, merchant and locksmith, speaks well of "the excellent art of carpentry" in his *Le Théâtre de l'Art de Charpentier Enriché de Divers Figures* (La Fleche, 1627). While Jousse dedicated the volume to *Le Haut et Puissant* Marquis de la Varenne—and manages to refer to Vitruvius—the largest part of that work is devoted to the design of elaborate roof framing and wooden domes, French style.

Back in England Primatt's title was picked up again in 1703 by Richard Neve who presented 283 pages on subjects arranged alphabetically from Abacus to Zoccolo.[16] While he paused to venerate such antiquarian concerns as Acroteria, Metops and Xylos, he did make many practical observations on current construction practices, along with a few quotations of unit prices. It is still, however, more a book for owners than builders or their journeymen and apprentices.

Then the "pattern book" business began to flourish. Designs for whole buildings were presented by British architects—authors such as Colin Campbell (1715), William Halfpenny (1724), William Kent (1727), Robert Morris (1728), James Gibbs (1728), Abraham Swan (1745), William Chambers (1757), William Pain (1758), James Stuart (1762), and Robert Adam (1764)[17]—to name the most important. Many of their books soon appeared in America and had a fairly wide use here. The Library Company of Philadelphia had some twenty-two works on "Civil Architecture" on its shelves in 1789 when its handsome new Hall, designed by the amateur William Thornton, was erected on Fifth Street. Seventeen house carpenters (mostly members of the CCCCP), eight bricklayers and a stone cutter, a plasterer, and a house painter took shares in the Library Company in lieu of wages,[18] testifying to the general thirst for published knowledge from the old country. The Carpenters' Company had its own library, but little is known about it in the eighteenth century.[19]

To consider the business of mensuration, some aspects of building practice common to England and her American colonies should be noted. No one has explained current procedure better than Sir Christopher Wren who, in a letter of 1681 to the Bishop of Oxford, discussed the methods of undertaking a construction project:

> There are three ways of working: by the Day, by Measure, By Great; if by the Day it tells me when they are Lazy. If by Measure it gives me light on every particular, and tells me what I am to provide. If by the Great I can make a sure bargain neither to be overreached nor to hurt the undertaker: for in things they are not every day used to, they doe often injure themselves, and when they begin to find it, they shuffle and slight the worke to save themselves. I think the best way in this businesse is to worke by measure: according to the prices in the Estimate or lower if you can, and measure the work at 3 or 4 measurements as it rises. But you must have an understanding trusty Measurer, ...[20]

Agreements for establishment of value by measure for work completed is what is involved in the Philadelphia book. Books of prices could also be used to estimate the cost of proposed work from quantities taken off of drawings; that is exactly what is done today by estimators using "unit prices." In the meantime, the method of establishing the cost of a work *after* construction, as practiced by members of the CCCCP using this book, has gone out of fashion.

As to American carpenters' price books earlier than 1786, there was one in Providence, Rhode Island (probably only in manuscript) begun in 1750.[21] The first printed example seems to be *The Carpenters' Rules of Work in the Town of Boston*, from the press of Mills and Hicks, School-street, 1774, a pamphlet of eleven pages. The present book may well be the second one printed but it was, as noted earlier, the first to include designs. After 1786 many were issued, and at places as far West as Peoria and St. Louis.

This brings us down to the present volume. By tradition, one of the first actions of the CCCCP after is founding, was to fix "a uniform scale of prices upon their work, so that the workman should receive a fair compensation for his labor, and the employer obtain a fair value for his money."[22] The earliest company records having been lost, it is no longer possible to trace the origin and first development of this important function.

By 1763 investment in the building site on Chestnut Street required that CCCCP business affairs be conducted with more fiscal responsibility. Thence forward, careful minutes were kept, and have survived under the care of the library of the American Philosophical Society.

One of the first Company actions noted in these minutes was the appointment of twelve of its members to the Committee on Prices of Work. These included Robert Smith, Gunning Bedford, Thomas Nevell and Benjamin Loxley, who were to play a leading part in the Company's affairs, especially during the construction of its new Hall. At the meeting of April 25, 1774, it was recorded that the Committee had worked out a set of revised prices, which was thereupon reviewed and adopted. The manuscript of the book was to be kept in the new Hall under the cognizance of the special committee. Members wishing to possess copies had to come to the Hall and make them personally.

In the meantime (1769) the Friendship Carpenters' Company of Philadelphia had been organized.[23] Working at the home of Samuel Clark (a room, fire and candles for two shillings per evening), they soon produced their own price book, a copy of which has been preserved in manuscript. But conflict arose with the pricing system of the older company and the men of Friendship tried to effect a working accommodation. In a rather obsequious letter dated January 15, 1770, they salute "their Elder Brethren" and refer to:

> the Reproach that has lain upon the Profession in a very general manner for some time past owing as they apprehend to the Different Methods used in Measuring and Valueing the work which belongs to it Cannot but desire to See some effectual means for removing such Scandal . . . .[24]

This attempt to share the mensuration techniques of the older company got them nowhere. In return, three months later, they received a condescending reply signed by Robert Smith which must have infuriated them:

> As to scandal or Reproach we [the CCCCP] for ourselves are not Sensible of any just cause for either, being conscious that the Methods for measuring and valueing we persue is more Equitable Expressive and satisfactory than any method ever practiced in this City before and many of us are Sensible that it is not Inferior to the best methods practis'd in any City within the King's Dominions . . . .[25]

This rebuff delayed efforts at conciliation for many years. In the meantime the Revolutionary War, in which members of the CCCCP and the Hall itself played a conspicuous part, came and went.

In the year 1785, two years after the signing of the Treaty of Paris, the Friendship Company was finally absorbed by the older one. Another committee of twelve was set up to prepare a new price book and to see it into print for the first time. This was done in the hope of answering complaints of prospective building owners, currently reluctant to pay higher prices for work. Costs in Philadelphia (so ran the explanation) had risen because of the increased elaboration of the buildings themselves as well as advancing costs of materials and labor.

Progress can be traced in the minutes of the special committee on prices and in the general *Account Book* of 1763–1834. On July 18, 1785, Thomas Nevell offered a set of "Plates representing diferent [sic] parts of Carpenters work . . . draughts necessary for the Engraver" at thirty-two dollars, his "first cost," and they were unanimously accepted. On December 12, it was voted to move to publication and the expenses were subsequently entered in the Company's books.[26] William Young got £34-7-6 for paper and Hall & Sellers, publishers of *The Pennsylvania Gazette*, £15 for printing the text. Thomas Bedwell, "Coper Plate Printer," a former partner of John Norman,[27] received £30-5-10 in several installments for engraving and printing the plates and Benjamin January £7-10-0 for binding the sheets. For the text, presumably acting as a scribe for the Committee, member Joseph Thornhill received £1-15-0. Undoubtedly each of the eighty-odd living members of the Company were presented with a copy of the new book though today less than a half dozen complete ones are known. In due course the 1786 edition was superceded by others dated 1805, 1831 and 1852.

Some years later another Philadelphia group, in protest against the CCCCP's "discriminate exclusion of persons," incorporated the "Practical House Carpenters' Society" and published in 1811 a *Book of Prices* dedicated to the citizens of Pennsylvania. It had fifty-eight pages of text, plus index, and eight engraved plates by Strickland.

A production of some size—but not of demonstrated originality—was the three-volume work of John Haviland (1792–1852), the English emigré, entitled *The Builders' Assistant*. Haviland designed some of Philadelphia's best buildings of the early nineteenth century. His book is embellished by sixty original designs on one hundred and fifty copper plates engraved by High Bridport. Bound in the third volume (1821) is a separate work entitled "House Carpenters' Book of Prices and Rules for Measuring and Valuing All Their Different Kinds of Work" dated 1819 and with thirty-one pages of prices. Also included is a "List of Prices of the Stone Masons & Bricklayers in Philadelphia" (eleven pages) and a "List of Prices of the Master Plasterers in Philadelphia" (three pages). Perhaps the most comprehensive American work of this class ever published was by architect James Gallier (1798–1868), *The American Builders' General Price Book and Estimator . . . to Elucidate the Principles of Ascertaining the Correct Value of Every Description of Artificers' Work Required in Building from the Prime Cost of Materials and Labour in Any Part of the United States.* The first edition, published in New York in 1833, has one hundred and twenty-eight pages of general text, seventy-two of Tables and Memoranda and seventeen of New York City "Laws Regulating Buildings." It was followed in 1834 and 1835 by new editions in Boston.

In 1836 Burns and Huddleston, Boston booksellers and stationers advertised that they kept constantly on hand "All kinds of Carpenters', Masons', Architects' and Builders' Price Books." Their Boston *Rules and Prices* book sold for fifty cents each or four dollars a dozen. A far cry from the close-held work we are publishing here!

NOTES

(1) for further discussion, *see* Charles E. Peterson, "Carpenters' Hall," *Transactions of the American Philosophical Society,* vol. 43, part 1 (Philadelphia, Penn., 1953), p. 105.

(2) Talbot Hamlin, *Benjamin Henry Latrobe* (New York, 1955), p. 147, note 1.

(3) Norman and Hall advertised in *The Pennsylvania Gazette* for August 17, 1774, as "Engravers and Drawing Masters" from London with architecture and copper-plate printing among their offerings. On May 11, 1775, Norman alone advertised for subscriptions to a work on Prussian military tactics with Thomas Nevell and Benjamin Loxley of the Carpenters' Company (among others) taking in subscriptions. By September 28, 1779, Norman was in business with Thomas Bedwell and selling coffins and paper hangings as well as engraving and printing. By 1783 he had gone to settle in Boston.

(4) Henry Russell Hitchcock, *American Architectural Books,* 3rd edition (Minneapolis, Minn., 1946), pp. iii, 103. David McNealy Stauffer, *American Engravers upon Copper and Steel* (New York, 1907), I, p. 191.

(5) RIBA Librarian John Harris has confirmed that no work has been done on these price books. Much the same situation, of course, prevails in America, except for the pioneering research of Professor Louise Hall.

(6) But in it is mentioned the fact that in the year 1799 the work had been "revised and regulated," indicating an earlier version.

(7) Republished in facsimile by Leonce Laget (Paris, 1967).

(8) The life and works of Nevell were outlined in Hannah Benner Roach, "Thomas Nevell (1721–1797), Carpenter, Educator, Patriot," *Journal of the Society of Architectural Historians* (May, 1965), vol. XXIV, no. 2, pp. 153–164.

(9) Charles E. Peterson, "Library Hall," *Historic Philadelphia* (Philadelphia, 1953), p. 146.

(10) Ernest Allen Connally, "Printed Books on Architecture 1485–1805," University of Illinois, 1960, p. 9.

(11) Sir John Summerson, speaking on BBC television, attempted to fill in the gaps between the differing authorities. *See* John Summerson, *The Classic Language of Architecture* (Cambridge, Mass., 1961), especially pp. 7–11. I suspect some of those early architects of laying booby traps for art historians.

(12) Alberti's pioneer work *De re Aedificatoria* was published in Florence in 1485.

(13) The 1703 edition of Moxon has just been republished by Praeger (New York, 1970) with Charles F. Montgomery and Benno M. Forman as editors. There are over a hundred pages on joinery and carpentry, two related and overlapping trades that never were clearly separated as to guild jurisdiction, in spite of extensive hearings before the Lord Mayor of London in the seventeenth century. The two trades did, however, unite in 1670 to keep the sawyers from organizing. *See* Edward Basil Jupp and William Willmer Pocock, *An Historical Account of the Worshipful Company of Carpenters of the City of London* (London, 1887), pp. 295–310.

(14) Preface to Moxon, 1677 edition.

(15) The beginnings of such organizations in England are obscure. In 1333 the Brotherhood of Carpenters of London drew up a book of ordinances which reveals that it was mainly a mutual welfare and burial society. By 1428/9 it had acquired a site for its hall and by 1455 it was clearly attempting to regulate trade in the capital. In the sixteenth century members were taking an active part in the civic and social life of the Livery Companies of the City and were conspicuous at royal funerals, coronations and other state affairs. *See* B. W. E. Alford and T. C. Barker, *A History of the Carpenters' Company* (London, 1968), pp. 16–19.

(16) Published under the pseudonym T. N. Philomath. The second

edition of 1726 has been printed in facsimile by Augustus M. Kelley (New York, 1969).

(17) List combined from Fiske Kimball, *Domestic Architecture of the American Colonies and of the Early Republic* (New York, 1922), pp. 58–60; and Connally, pp. 36, 37.

(18) Peterson, "Library Hall," pp. 134, 135, 146. Some of this impressive cooperation may have been due to the mechanics' close association with Benjamin Franklin, founder of the Library Company and close political ally during the Revolution.

(19) There has long been a tradition that James Portues who died in the 1730's, bequeathed his books to the Company and that the first volume purchased was acquired in 1737.

(20) Frank Jenkins, *Architect and Patron* (London, New York and Toronto, 1961), pp. 128, 129. Professor Jenkins discusses this subject on pages 143–145 and cites the sarcastic little volume by James MacPacke, "Bricklayer's Labourer," *Oikidia; or Nutshells.* This was published in London in 1785, the year before the present volume, and a copy was listed as on the shelves of the Library Company of Philadelphia four years later.

(21) *Rules for House Carpenters Work in the Town of Providence* (Providence, R. I., 1796), p. 2.

(22) 1866, p. 128.

(23) November 18, 1769 at a meeting in the Union Library. *Minutes of the Friendship Carpenters' Company, 1769–1775.* Bound mss., Papers of the CCCCP at the American Philosophical Society Library.

(24) *Ibid.*, May 28, 1770.

(25) *Ibid.*, August 20, 1770. This exchange certainly reveals the high regard in which the price book was held.

(26) Bound mss. for the period 1763–1834. The entries mentioned here run from 7 mo. 3, 1786 to 6 mo. 16, 1787.

(27) The copper plates from which the illustrations were printed are preserved at Carpenters' Hall. On the reverse of some are engravings which had been used by John Norman to illustrate earlier works. Bedwell appears in Biddle's 1791 directory as a "hanging paper manufacturer" at 234 North Front Street and in Hardie's 1794 directory as a "manufacturer of the extract of bark" at the same address.

List of Names (pp. iii–iv)
The list carries the names of one hundred and thirty-three members of the Company. Fifty-one of them were noted (by asterisk) as deceased, leaving a total of eighty-two presumably active in 1786. Twenty-seven of these had been members of the Friendship Company, merged into the earlier association in that same year. It is not known how the list was compiled or if it is actually complete, the records of the Company going back only to the year 1763. As long ago as 1866 the first ten names on the list were identified as the "original associators."* The roll now signed by members at the time of admission begins with Joseph ffox (d. 1780) and this year (1971), reached the number 639.

Introduction (pp. v–vii)
A longhand version of this essay has been preserved among the company's manuscripts. It had to be much improved as to diction and spelling before type was set.

The Articles (pp. vii–xii)
The fifteen articles were meant to establish the order of regular business and assign the duties of the various officers. They are self-explanatory.

The Table (pp. xiii–xv)
This was intended to help estimators with the arithmetically complicated business of surface measurement using the English monetary units of shilling and pence as related to measures of yards, feet and inches.

The Rules, Ordinances and Bye-Laws (pp. xvii–xxi)
Found in most copies, they are omitted in this facsimile. They were obviously inserted by a binder only after incorporation of the company by the Pennsylvania Legislature on April 2, 1790. The new articles were intended to supercede those printed above and had to be made eight years after the date (1786) of the title page.

Frontispiece plates
Those of Carpenters' Hall, plan and elevation, were originally paired but appear separately in this edition. The other copper plates are here numbered—for the first time—with Roman numerals I–XXXV and each is accompanied by an explanatory note.

An Act to Incorporate the Carpenters' Company . . . together with Reminiscences of The Hall . . . and Catalogue of Books in the Library (Philadelphia, 1866), p. 78.

The Rules for Measuring and Valuing House-Carpenters Work (pp. 1–44)

Forty-four printed pages devoted to mensuration and valuation make up the bulk of the book. The order of arrangement follows the procedure of the builder, that is, it starts with the making of plans and continues with the framing of roofs, floors and partitions, treats of doors, windows, partitions, stairways and trimming out generally, prices various types of fencing and even considers such specialties as pulpits and cisterns for distilleries. It ends up with the fine points of Tuscan, Doric, Ionic, Corinthian and Composite ordonnance, noting the alternate methods of turning and boring columns from solid logs versus the gluing up of pieces to make the whole. Each item is described as to type and size and blanks are provided for entering unit prices in longhand (many of which appear in this edition). The latter were obviously expected to vary from time to time (mostly to go up, as they do today).

The builders' terms used in that period are not completely understood today. It should be remembered that the building trades were not generally under the cognizance of literary men. The carpenters' vocabulary was learned on the job by the apprentice—not out of books. This resulted in local names for things which would, in many cases, be more or less incomprehensible to other carpenters only a hundred miles away. In addition, both spelling and pronunciation were far from standardized and that is still true, though to a lesser degree, today.

Drawings (i–xxv)

According to the "Rules" the drawing of designs was to be charged by the carpenter "in proportion to the trouble." Unfortunately original architectural drawings from the eighteenth century are very scarce today. There were far fewer of them to start with and they were probably worn out on the job by the foreman, there being no such thing as the modern convenience of blueprint copies. The originals, on heavy handmade paper, would not fold readily into packets like contemporary letters handed down to us, neatly bound in red tapes. The few originals still available for study are far simpler than the drawings made today. Not much detail was needed, for the carpenter was trained to carry through the business of "trimming out" a building according to generally accepted and well understood techniques. He was allowed a certain amount of artistic initiative and discretion and the attractive character of the finished results justified the confidence placed in him.

The "trouble" incurred in each case would depend on the amount of special detail provided—or, say, the number of alternative designs the owner wanted to see before making a decision. In any case, the charges were not high, to judge by the bill of Edmund Woolley (himself a member of the CCCCP) who was paid on July 22, 1736 only five pounds for drawing the plans and elevations of the Pennsylvania State House.* Now called Independence Hall, it was always considered one of the grandest public buildings in the American colonies. Woolley's drawings have been lost, as have those of the better known Robert Smith who designed Carpenters' Hall.

The latter was what historians today call a carpenter-architect but he had a very wide practice, making plans for projects scattered all the way from Virginia to Rhode Island. While we have mention of a public exhibition of Smith's drawings (some years after his death in 1777) with one possible exception—a rough sheet related to the Eastern State Hospital in Williamsburg, probably 1770—all have disappeared. We do have the 1786 engravings, presumably made from Smith's plan and front elevation of Carpenters' Hall which appear as frontispiece in this edition. An elevation of Smith's Christ Church, Philadelphia, steeple (built 1758), probably also engraved from the architect's drawing, has been preserved in the form of a copper plate in a book by Owen Biddle (CCCCP member 1800–1807), *The Young Carpenters' Assistant* (Philadelphia, 1805).

*Charles E. Peterson, "Early Architects of Independence Hall," American Notes, *JSAH*, vol. XI, no. 3 (October, 1952), p. 23. They are probably not the working drawings from which the structure was built.

ARTICLES

OF THE

CARPENTERS COMPANY

OF

PHILADELPHIA:

AND THEIR

RULES

FOR MEASURING AND VALUING

HOUSE-CARPENTERS WORK.

PHILADELPHIA: PRINTED BY HALL AND SELLERS.

M,DCC,LXXXVI.

LIST OF NAMES

OF THE

Carpenters Company

OF

PHILADELPHIA.

Note. Thofe marked with an Afterifk [*] are deceafed.

JOSEPH Henmarfh, *
  James Portues, *
Samuel Powel, *
Jacob Ufher, *
Edmond Woolley, *
Jofeph Harrifon, *
John Nichols, *
John Harrifon, *
Benjamin Clark, *
Ifaac Zane,
William Clark, *
Edward Warner, *
Samuel Rhoads, *
Reefe Lloyd, *
Jofeph Rakeftraw, *
Tobias Grifcom, *
John Mifflin,
William Coleman, *
John Price, *
Jofeph Hitchcock, *
Jacob Lewis, *
Jofeph Fox, *
Jofeph Thornhill,
John Thornhill, *

Robert Smith, *
Benjamin Loxley,
James Worrell,
John Goodwin, *
Abraham Carlile, *
James Davis, *
Ellis Price, *
Gunning Bedford,
Thomas Nevell,
James Armitage,
Samuel Grifcom,
James Pearfon,
John Wayne, *
William Roberts,
Levi Budd,
George Plim, junior, *
Ifaac Lefever, *
Richard Armitt,
James Potter,
Benjamin Mifflin, *
George Wood,
Ezekiel Worrell, *
Jofiah Harper, *
Jofeph Rakeftraw,

Silas

Silas Engles,
Joseph Rush, *
Joseph Rhoads, *
Isaac Coats, *
Patrick Craghead, *
William Dilworth, *
Robert Carson, *
William Rakestraw, *
John Hitchcock, *
Joshua Pancoast, *
Lawrence Rice, *
Evan Peters, *
William Lownes,
Samuel Powel,
Joseph Gridley, *
William Robinson,
James Bringhurst,
James Graysbury,
Jacob Reary, *
Thomas Shoemaker,
David Evans,
William Colliday,
Abraham Jones, *
Thomas Middleton, *
William Boyer, *
William Ashton,
John Trip, *
Andrew Edge, *
Samuel Jervis,
Samuel Wallis,
Matthew M'Glathery,
Moses Thomas,
John Allen, *
Thomas Procter,
Adam Zantzinger,
John Keen,
John Lort,
Joseph Govett,
Joseph Ogilby,
William Williams,
Robert Allison,
George Forepaugh,
Samuel M'Clure,

John Smith,
Matthias Sadler,
James Gibson,
George Ingels,
Frazer Kinsley,
James Corkrin,
Joseph Rakestraw, junior,
Joseph Thornhill, junior,
John King,
Andrew Boyd,
Conrad Bartling,
William Garrigues,
John Rugan,
Mark Rodes,
Robert Evans,
Joseph Wetherell,
Hugh Roberts,
Isaac Jones,
Samuel Pancoast,
Matthias Val Keen,
William Stevenson,
Robert Morrell,
Richard Mosley,
John Reinhard,
Samuel Pastorius,
John Barker,
Josiah Matlack,
John Piles,
Joseph Clark,
William Zane,
Benjamin Mitchell,
Thomas Savery,
Nathan Allen Smith,
Samuel Tolbert,
Samuel Jones,
John Hall,
Joseph Howell, junior,
Israel Hallowell,
John Harrison,
Ebenezer Ferguson,
John Donohue,
John Cooper.

INTRO-

INTRODUCTION.

AS Pennſylvania is in a ſtate of infancy with regard to Europe, conſequently arts and improvements amongſt its inhabitants are the more neceſſary, and ſuch as are moſt uſeful ſhould doubt-leſs be the firſt object of their care.

ARCHITECTURE, or the ART OF BUILDING, among other im-provements, ſhould not be neglected, eſpecially where ſtrength, convenience and elegance are joined in the ſtructure of a building. In the city of Philadelphia, where many thouſands are annually expended for that purpoſe, it may be uſeful to make ſome obſer-vations reſpecting the difference between ſeveral edifices that have been erected in and near the ſaid city within theſe few years, and thoſe plain ſimple buildings which were erected in the early times of this ſtate, to ſerve the neceſſary purpoſes of life, which houſes were plain and ſimple, the different parts nearly the ſame labour. Buildings of convenience ſucceeded thoſe, in proportion as the in-habitants grew more opulent, and ſtrangers from time to time arrived from other countries, where many elegancies were in uſe; thus ſuch improvements were made in the mode of building, as made it neceſſary to alter the method of meaſuring, or raiſe the price of different parts of work in the ſame houſe, that the car-penter might be paid for his labour. Both were done, but gene-rally they altered the method of taking dimenſions, by adding to

ſome

some parts one half (more than the superficial dimensions) doubling or trebling others, and sometimes oftner, where there was more labour in the performance, and the price was set on the general and not on the particular parts of the work. This was equity, but seldom gave satisfaction ; because there was a greater number of squares in the bill, than were superficially contained in the work that was measured.

Many gentlemen who have had houses lately built, for want of being properly informed of the difference between such plain houses as aforesaid and such as they themselves have had built, have been dissatisfied, expecting their work should be at the same price per square, and measured in the same manner, as has been customary for plainer buildings. But this was unreasonable, because those gentlemen must be sensible that the form of the work done in their buildings, and the labour required in the performance, is very different from that done in such plain houses as those aforementioned,

Other reasons that may be offered, why the prices on carpenters work should be altered, are—that men could live thirty years ago with two thirds of the expence that they can at present, and journeymens wages were at one fourth less than is now given.

The stuff also used at this time is certainly from one sixth to one eighth more labour than that used some years ago, it being in general so much worse—and to expect work now, under all these and many other disadvantages, for the same price by the square that the workmen had then, can hardly be deemed equitable or just.

These difficulties were taken into consideration by a number of reputable carpenters, who appointed twelve of their company, as a committee, to consider of the several parts of carpentry, and set a price on every particular part, according to the mode of finishing, either by the square, yard or foot.

Notwith-

Notwithſtanding all the pains that hath been taken to aſcertain the true value of every part of our buſineſs, yet there are many parts that bear the ſame name, and perhaps near the ſame ſize and likeneſs with others, that are of more or leſs value. Therefore it is highly neceſſary, and we earneſtly deſire (knowing that juſtice is not likely to be done without judgment) that all perſons concerned in building, take care to employ ſuch men to meaſure as are able to judge, and do know what is the meaning of the terms and deſcriptions of the following works.

As there is ſuch great variety in the building buſineſs, we think it almoſt impoſſible to deſcribe by words every part, in ſuch a manner that any one may underſtand, unleſs they are well acquainted with the art of building. And as to the following prices, fixed to the ſeveral parts of carpentry, we deſire all thoſe that may hereafter be concerned to take particular notice, that ſuch prices are judged to be the value of the following articles, when they are done in a ſubſtantial, neat, workmanlike manner. And if any part is done otherwiſe, we deſire that the price may be lowered, at the diſcretion of thoſe that are good judges.

The real intent and meaning of what hath been done is, that every gentleman concerned in building may have the value of his money, and that every workman may have the worth of his labour.

ARTICLES

ARTICLES

OF THE

CARPENTERS COMPANY.

THE Carpenters Company of the city and county of Philadelphia having for many years met together, for preferving
good order among ourfelves, and for the utility and benefit of our
fellow-citizens, and having for that end from time to time made
fundry articles, do now agree to the following:

ARTICLE I. That we will meet together on the third Monday
(or fecond day of the week) in January, April, July and October, in every year, at the Hall, or fuch other place as the Company may direct, and if any member fhall neglect to attend
within one hour after the time appointed, he fhall forfeit Six-
pence; and not meeting the whole evening, fhall pay One Shilling fine; alfo every member, at each quarterly meeting, fhall
pay One Shilling into the ftock, for relief of the poor and other
incident charges; and whatfoever fhall be expended at each meeting fhall be paid by the members met.

ARTICLE II. That at our annual meetings in January in every
year we will choofe, by ballot, a Prefident, who, at the meetings
of the Company, fhall regulate our debates, and ftate the proper
queftions

queſtions when any matter is to be determined ; and have the
caſting vote ; and cauſe ſuch entries to be made, as ſhall be agreeable thereto : He ſhall keep in his cuſtody all the monies, books,
papers and effeɛts of the Company, not otherwiſe diſpoſed of ;
and pay ſuch of the monies depoſited in his hands as ſhall be di-
reɛted by the Company at their ſeveral meetings ; and, at leaſt one
week before the annual meeting in every year, ſhall ſettle his accounts with the committee choſen for that purpoſe ; and at the
expiration of his office (if he is not re-eleɛted) ſhall pay and de-
liver unto the ſucceeding Preſident, all the monies, books and
effeɛts belonging to the Company, in his hands.

Article III. And whereas there are now three Aſſiſtants in
office, and the term of ſervice of the eldeſt expires at the annual meeting, and at that time another ſhall be choſen to ſerve
for three years. Their duty ſhall be to adviſe with the Preſident
in all things relating to the Company ; they ſhall take care the
accounts are duly ſettled ; that all. theſe articles are punɛtually
obſerved ; and aſſiſt the preſident in preſerving due decorum at all
the meetings of the Company. The eldeſt of them who is pre-
ſent ſhall preſide in the abſence of the Preſident.

Article IV. Whereas the ſervice of the Company requires
there ſhould be three Wardens, therefore it is agreed, that at
every annual meeting a member ſhall be choſen for that office, to
continue therein for three years. Their duty ſhall be jointly to
warn the members to meet at ſuch time and place as ſhall be di-
reɛted by the Company, by notices in writing, left at their re-
ſpeɛtive dwellings before one o'clock of the day appointed for
meeting, under the penalty of Six-pence for each member ſo ne-
gleɛted ; and at every meeting to colleɛt all the arrears of fines
due to the Company, receive the quarterages and entrance money
paid by the members ; they ſhall keep a book containing a liſt of
the names of all the Company, and enter in the ſame book all the
money they ſhall colleɛt in their wardenſhip, and pay the ſame

b   to to the Prefident immediately after each meeting, taking his receipt in faid book.

ARTICLE V. Any perfon chofen into office agreeable to thefe articles refufing to ferve, fhall forfeit and pay to the Company Five Shillings, except the Warden, who fhall pay Ten Shillings, unlefs he has already ferved. If any officer dies within the term of his office, his place fhall be fupplied at the next quarterly meeting.

ARTICLE VI. Whenever there is a confiderable fum of money belonging to the Company in poffeffion of the Prefident, he, with the Affiftants, or any two of them, fhall put the fame to interest, taking fufficient real fecurity (the title approved of by Counfel learned in the law) in the name of the Prefident and Affiftants, jointly and feverally, for the ufe of the Company.

ARTICLE VII. Every member of this Company hereby engages, that he will not enter into or undertake work begun by any other member, until the firft undertaker is fatisfied for the work done, unlefs by his or their confent. Any member tranfgreffing this article, and it being duly proved before the Prefident and one or more of the Affiftants and any five members, fhall pay to the firft undertaker fuch fum as they fhall judge reafonable. Provided always, and it is hereby agreed, That no member, through negligence or delay, caufes his employer to fuffer, for want of that difpatch which might be reafonably made. In this cafe, the Prefident (on application of the employer or any perfon on his behalf) fhall immediately fummon the Affiftants, and as many of the Company as he fhall judge neceffary, who fhall take the premifes into confideration, and affign the employer fuch relief as they fhall think neceffary. And if any member fhall refufe or neglect to obferve fuch directions of the Prefident, &c. the cafe fhall be laid before the Company at their next meeting, who will take fuch order thereon as to them fhall appear reafonable.

ARTICLE

[**xi**]

ARTICLE VIII. If a difference arifes between any of the members relative to the trade, the perfon who thinks himfelf aggrieved is enjoined to apply to the Prefident, who, with the Affiftants, fhall endeavour to accommodate the affair; but if their efforts prove ineffectual, the parties are at liberty each of them to chufe two members of the Company, the Prefident and Affiftants to name another member, in addition to the four fo chofen, and thofe perfons, or any three of them, are to determine the affair, and report their proceedings to the Prefident, for the information of the parties, who are required to acquiefce in the determination of the faid referees.

ARTICLE IX. Any member, widow, or minor children of a member, being by accident or ficknefs reduced to want, making application to the Prefident, he, in conjunction with the Affiftants, may relieve him, her or them, at their difcretion, until the next quarterly meeting; and then fhall lay a ftate of their circumftances before the faid meeting, who fhall determine what may be further neceffary to be done.

ARTICLE X. After the deceafe of any member of this Company, leaving a fon of the fame trade, fuch fon, being approved of by the Company, may be admitted a member without paying any entrance money.

ARTICLE XI. And for the prefervation of good order at our feveral meetings, it is agreed that no perfon fhall introduce any fubject of converfation foreign to the intention of the meeting, until the bufinefs is done; and that no more than one perfon fhall fpeak at a time, ftanding up, and addreffing himfelf to the Prefident; nor fhall fpeak more than twice to one queftion, without leave firft given.

ARTICLE XII. Any perfon being chofen a member of this Company, having proper notice thereof, and neglecting to attend

b 2

for

for two fucceffive ftated meetings after his election, pay his entrance, and fign thefe articles (unlefs ficknefs or fome other fufficient reafon be given to the Company) fhall not be deemed a member, unlefs he is re-elected.

ARTICLE XIII. If any member takes a flave apprentice, he fhall pay to the Prefident, for the ufe of the Company, Twenty Pounds; or hire a flave as a journeyman, fhall pay the fum of One Dollar for every month that he employs him, for the ufe aforefaid.

ARTICLE XIV. Laftly, If any member refufes to pay fines wherewith he fhall be charged, or his quarterages, or otherwife difregards thefe articles, he fhall be deemed unworthy to be a member of this Company, and his name erafed out of the book.

A TABLE

A TABLE of the fractional Parts of a Yard of Wainscot, &c. from 1s. to 25s.

1 yard.		6 feet.			½ yard.			3 feet.			1 foot.			9 inch.			6 inch.			3 inch.		
s.	d.	s.	d.	q.	s.	d.	q.	s.	d.	q.	s.	d.	q.	s.	d.	q.	s.	d.	q.	s.	d.	q.
1	0		8			6			4		1	1		1				2			1	
1	3		10			7	2		5		1	2		1	1			3			1	
1	6	1	0			9			6		2			1	2		1				2	
1	9	1	2			10	2		7		2	1		1	3		1				2	
2	0	1	4		1	0			8		2	2		2			1	1			2	
2	3	1	6		1	1	2		9		3			2	1		1	2			3	
2	6	1	8		1	3			10		3	1		2	2		1	2			3	
2	9	1	10		1	4	2		11		3	2		2	3		1	3			3	
3	0	2	0		1	6		1			4			3			2			1		
3	3	2	2		1	7	2	1	1		4	1		3	1		2			1		
3	6	2	4		1	9		1	2		4	2		3	2		2	1		1		
3	9	2	6		1	10	2	1	3		5			3	3		2	2		1	1	
4	0	2	8		2			1	4		5	1		4			2	2		1	1	
4	3	2	10		2	1	2	1	5		5	2		4	1		2	3		1	1	
4	6	3	0		2	3		1	6		6			4	2		3			1	2	
4	9	3	2		2	4	2	1	7		6	1		4	3		3			1	2	
5	0	3	4		2	6		1	8		6	2		5			3	1		1	2	
5	3	3	6		2	7	2	1	9		7			5	1		3	2		1	3	
5	6	3	8		2	9		1	10		7	1		5	2		3	2		1	3	
5	9	3	10		2	10	2	1	11		7	2		5	3		3	3		1	3	
6	0	4	0		3			2			8			6			4			2		
6	3	4	2		3	1	2	2	1		8	1		6	1		4			2		
6	6	4	4		3	3		2	2		8	2		6	2		4	1		2		
6	9	4	6		3	4	2	2	3		9			6	3		4	2		2	1	
7	0	4	8		3	6		2	4		9	1		7			4	2		2	1	
7	3	4	10		3	7	2	2	5		9	2		7	1		4	3		2	1	
7	6	5	0		3	9		2	6		10			7	2		5			2	2	
7	9	5	2		3	10	2	2	7		10	1		7	3		5			2	2	
8	0	5	4		4			2	8		10	2		8			5	1		2	2	
8	3	5	6		4	1	2	2	9		11			8	1		5	2		2	3	
8	6	5	8		4	3		2	10		11	1		8	2		5	2		2	3	
8	9	5	10		4	4	2	2	11		11	2		8	3		5	3		2	3	
9	0	6	0		4	6		3			1	0		9			6			3		
9	3	6	2		4	7	2	3	1		1	0	1	9	1		6			3		
9	6	6	4		4	9		3	2		1	0	2	9	2		6	1		3		
9	9	6	6		4	10	2	3	3		1	1		9	3		6	2		3	1	

A TABLE, &c.

1 yard.	6 feet.	½ yard.	3 feet.	1 foot.	9 inch.	6 inch.	3 inch.
s. d.	s. d.	s. d. q.	s. d. q.	s. d. q.	s. d. q.	s. d. q.	s. d. q.
10 0	6 8	5	3 4	1 1 1	10	6 2	3 1
10 3	6 10	5 1 2	3 5	1 1 2	10 1	6 3	3 1
10 6	7 0	5 3	3 6	1 2	10 2	7	3 2
10 9	7 2	5 4 2	3 7	1 2 1	10 3	7	3 2
11 0	7 4	5 6	3 8	1 2 2	11	7 1	3 2
11 3	7 6	5 7 2	3 9	1 3	11 1	7 2	3 3
11 6	7 8	5 9	3 10	1 3 1	11 2	7 2	3 3
11 9	7 10	5 10 2	3 11	1 3 2	11 3	7 3	3 3
12 0	8	6	4	1 4	1	8	4
12 3	8 2	6 1 2	4 1	1 4 1	1　1	8	4
12 6	8 4	6 3	4 2	1 4 2	1　2	8 1	4
12 9	8 6	6 4 2	4 3	1 5	1　3	8 2	4 1
13 0	8 8	6 6	4 4	1 5 1	1 1	8 2	4 1
13 3	8 10	6 7 2	4 5	1 5 2	1 1 1	8 3	4 1
13 6	9	6 9	4 6	1 6	1 1 2	9	4 2
13 9	9 2	6 10 2	4 7	1 6 1	1 1 3	9	4 2
14 0	9 4	7	4 8	1 6 2	1 2	9 1	4 2
14 3	9 6	7 1 2	4 9	1 7	1 2 1	9 2	4 3
14 6	9 8	7 3	4 10	1 7 1	1 2 2	9 2	4 3
14 9	9 10	7 4 2	4 11	1 7 2	1 2 3	9 3	4 3
15 0	10	7 6	5	1 8	1 3	10	5
15 3	10 2	7 7 2	5 1	1 8 1	1 3 1	10	5
15 6	10 4	7 9	5 2	1 8 2	1 3 2	10 1	5
15 9	10 6	7 10 2	5 3	1 9	1 3 3	10 2	5 1
16 0	10 8	8	5 4	1 9 1	1 4	10 2	5 1
16 3	10 10	8 1 2	5 5	1 9 2	1 4 1	10 3	5 1
16 6	11	8 3	5 6	1 10	1 4 2	11	5 2
16 9	11 2	8 4 2	5 7	1 10 1	1 4 3	11	5 2
17 0	11 4	8 6	5 8	1 10 2	1 5	11 1	5 2
17 3	11 6	8 7 2	5 9	1 11	1 5 1	11 2	5 3
17 6	11 8	8 9	5 10	1 11 1	1 5 2	11 2	5 3
17 9	11 10	8 10 2	5 11	1 11 2	1 5 3	11 3	5 3
18 0	12	9	6	2	1 6	1	6
18 3	12 2	9 1 2	6 1	2　　1	1 6 1	1	6
18 6	12 4	9 3	6 2	2　　2	1 6 2	1 1	6
18 9	12 6	9 4 2	6 3	2 1	1 6 3	1 2	6 1
19 0	12 8	9 6	6 4	2 1 1	1 7	1 2	6 1
19 3	12 10	9 7 2	6 5	2 1 2	1 7 1	1 3	6 1

A TABLE, &c.

1 yard.			6 feet.			½ yard.			3 feet.			1 foot.			9 inch.			6 inch.			3 inch.		
s.	d.	q.	s.	d.		s.	d.	q.	s.	d.	q.	s.	d.	q.	s.	d.	q.	s.	d.	q.	s.	d.	q.
19	6		13			9	9		6	6		2	2		1	7	2	1	1		6	2	
19	9		13	2		9	10	2	6	7		2	2	1	1	7	3	1	1		6	2	
20	0		13	4		10			6	8		2	2	2	1	8		1	1	1	6	2	
20	3		13	6		10	1	2	6	9		2	3		1	8	1	1	1	2	6	3	
20	6		13	8		10	3		6	10		2	3	1	1	8	2	1	1	2	6	3	
20	9		13	10		10	4	2	6	11		2	3	2	1	8	3	1	1	3	6	3	
21	0		14			10	6		7			2	4		1	9		1	2		7		
21	3		14	2		10	7	2	7	1		2	4	1	1	9	1	1	2		7		
21	6		14	4		10	9		7	2		2	4	2	1	9	2	1	2	1	7		
21	9		14	6		10	10	2	7	3		2	5		1	9	3	1	2	2	7	1	
22	0		14	8		11			7	4		2	5	1	1	10		1	2	2	7	1	
22	3		14	10		11	1	2	7	5		2	5	2	1	10	1	1	2	3	7	1	
22	6		15			11	3		7	6		2	6		1	10	2	1	3		7	2	
22	9		15	2		11	4	2	7	7		2	6	1	1	10	3	1	3		7	2	
23	0		15	4		11	6		7	8		2	6	2	1	11		1	3	1	7	2	
23	3		15	6		11	7	2	7	9		2	7		1	11	1	1	3	2	7	3	
23	6		15	8		11	9		7	10		2	7	1	1	11	2	1	3	2	7	3	
23	9		15	10		11	10	2	7	11		2	7	2	1	11	3	1	3	3	7	3	
24	0		16			12			8			2	8		2			1	4		8		
24	3		16	2		12	1	2	8	1		2	8	1	2		1	1	4		8		
24	6		16	4		12	3		8	2		2	8	2	2		2	1	4	1	8		
24	9		16	6		12	4	2	8	3		2	9		2		3	1	4	2	8	1	
25	0		16	8		12	6		8	4		2	9	1	2	1		1	4	2	8	1	

Note. All Fractions less than a Farthing are omitted in the foregoing Table.

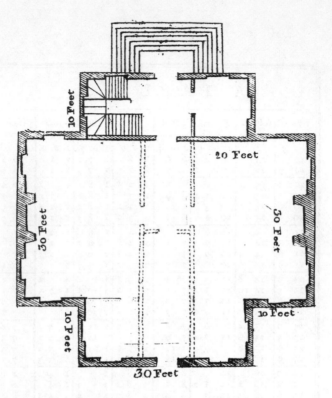

Carpenters' Hall, plan. Probably engraved from architect Robert Smith's original drawings, now lost. The unusual cross-shaped floor plan seems, by the dotted lines, to have been originally divided into smaller areas. But these may have been intended to represent the second-floor layout.

R U L E S

HOUSE-CARPENTERS WORK.

D RAWING Defigns, making out Bills of Scantling, col-
lecting Materials, and fticking up Stuff, are to be charged
by the Carpenter in proportion to the trouble.

To take the dimenfions of floors of joifts in brick buildings add
nine inches, and in ftone twelve inches, more than the clear of
the walls on the fide the joifts bear on.

In frame buildings meafure to the ends of the joifts by the clear
the other way.

R O O F S. Take the length from the top of the rafter to the
back of the cornice, if pieced out; and if not, to the toe of
the rafter. If the laths are fupported with pieces to nail the
barge-board to, meafure to the outfide of the walls, otherwife
in the clear.

In frame buildings, take the fuperficial dimenfions of the fides and
ends, the collar-beams to be meafured on the under-fide, to the
outfide of the rafter.

In taking dimenfions of partitions, add three inches to the height
of the ftory for nailing.

A   CEILING

	£.	s.	d.

CEILING Joists, without floors on them, from 4
to 6 inches deep, per square, from 4/ to   6 —

SLEEPERS for cellars or ftores, and framed floors
of joift not exceeding 8 inches deep (without girders) or roofs of fmall buildings, alfo ftables and
fhops, the pofts about 6 inches, and the fills 6 or
7 inches, per fquare, from   5/ to   -   -   7 —

If framed with hewed ftuff, per fquare, from 7/ to   9 —

> *Note.* The ftuff fuppofed to be hewed by fome
> other perfon.

FRAMING floors of joifts, of 9 inches deep, per
fquare,   -   -   -   -   -   8 —

Ditto, 10 inches deep, per fquare,   -   -   9 —

Ditto, 11 inches deep, per fquare,   -   -   10 —

Ditto, 12 inches deep, per fquare,   -   -   11 6

Ditto, 13 inches deep, per fquare,   -   -   12 6

Ditto, 14 inches deep, per fquare,   -   -   14 —

And in proportion, if deeper.

> *Note.* Thefe joifts are fuppofed from 13 to 14
> inches in the clear; but if nearer together, or
> further apart, the price to be in proportion.
>
> If joifts are double tufked, when there is only
> one girder, add one fourth of the above prices
> to every fquare of framing, and in proportion
> where there are more girders.
>
> If floors are bridged, add two thirds of the afore-
> faid prices for the extra work, and if there are
> ceiling joifts, add per fquare,   -   -   10

FRAMING or trimming over cellar doors or windows in any of the foregoing floors, charge from
one third to one fourth of the price to every fquare,
for each door or window fo framed.   GIRD-

	£.	s.	d.
GIRDERS of 7 inches deep, per foot running,	-	-	8
but if two or more, per foot, - -	-	-	9
Ditto 8 inches deep, per foot, - -	-	-	9
if two or more, per foot, - -	-	-	10
Ditto 9 inches deep, per foot, - -	-	-	10
if two or more, per foot, - -	-	-	11
Ditto 10 inches deep, per foot, - -	-	-	11·½
if two or more, per foot, - -	-	1	1
Ditto 11 inches deep, per foot, - -	-	1	2
if two or more, per foot, - -	-	1	4
Ditto 12 inches deep, per foot, - -	-	1	4
if two or more, per foot, - -	-	1	6
Ditto 13 inches deep, per foot, - -	-	1	6½
if two or more, per foot, - -	-	1	9
Ditto 14, 15, 16, 17 or 18 inches deep, per foot,			
from 1/9 to - -	-	2	6
if two or more, per foot, 2/ - 10 -	-	3	-
If any of those girders are truss'd, add per foot,	-	1	6
And if bolted, add per foot more, - -	-	-	2

Note. If girders are framed edgeways, measure
them on the edge, or as deep as the joists, if
they exceed the narrow way of the girder.

If girders are planed or chamfered, value according to the work.

	£.	s.	d.
FRAME houses or stores, full studded, fit for plai- stering, per square, - -	-	10	-
WALL plates and raising-pieces, measured side and edge by their length, per square, from 10/ to	-	15	-

FRAMING

| | £. | s. | d. |

FRAMING roofs, with collar-beams of small scantling, from 4 to 6 inches in the middle of the rafter and 3 inches thick, and about 20 inches distant, per square, from 7/ to - - - 10 ~

Ditto rafters, from 6 to 7 inches in the middle, by 3 and a half inches thick, and about 18 inches apart, per square, - - ~ 12 ~

Roofs framed with two collar-beams and short rafters on the top, and a board nailed from the lower collar-beam to the top of the rafter, the lower rafters 6 and a half or 7 inches in the middle, by 3 and a half inches thick, per square, - ~ 15 ~

The boards to be the same price per foot running.

ROOFS framed with principals and purlins, a collar-beam to each principal (the collar-beams measured side and edge by their length) per square, 1 ~ ~

Roofs framed with principal beams, king-posts, braces and purlins, the principal rafters at 9 or 10 feet distance, measure the outside as before; but to measure the internal framing, take the length of the principal beam A B, by half the perpendicular height from the top of the beam, then add the depth of the beam for the height, per square, 1 6 ~

If the floor is framed suitable for boarding, measure as usual.

If ceiling-joists only, charge them, per square, ~ 10 ~

ROOFS

R O O F S framed with king-posts, collar-beams, hammer-beams, braces and purlins, each principal at 9 or 10 feet distance, extending from 40 to 45 feet, per square,   -   -   -   -   *1 10 -*

If such roofs span 60 feet, per square,   -   -   *1 17 6*

The wall-plates at the same price.

> To measure the above described roofs, take the superficial contents of the outside framing; and to measure the internal framing, take the length of the back of the rafter by the length of the line A B, drawn at right angles from the back of the rafter to the lower edge of the collar-beam, under the middle of the king-post.

> *Note.* Each principal in the last described roof is supposed to have one king-post, but if more are required, there must be an addition to the price.

F R A M I N G arched ceilings to the foregoing roofs, per square,   -   -   -   *1 - -*

If there are groins in the ceilings, they are to be measured superficial, at double the aforesaid prices.

If there are hips or valleys in the foregoing roofs, charge them at double the foregoing prices.

> *Note.* All scaffolding, necessary for raising the above roofs, to be charged for by the time spent thereat.

N E W Lathing and shingling with 3 feet shingles, 11 inch courses, per square,   -   -   *- 12 -*

Ditto,

	£.	s.	d.
Ditto, 10 inch courses, per square,		13	~
Ditto, 9 inch courses, per square,		14	~
Ditto, 8 inch courses, per square,		15	~
Ditto, 7 inch courses, per square,		16	6
Ditto, with 2 feet shingles, 7 inch courses, per square,		18	~
Ditto, 6 inch courses, per square,	1	~	~
Ditto, 5¼ inch courses, per square,	1	1	~
Lathing and shingling with 18 inch shingles, 5 inches wide, 4¼ inch courses, per square,	1	6	~
Ditto, 4 inch courses, per square,	1	10	~
And with the common 18 inch shingles, 4¼ inch courses, per square,	1	10	~
Ditto, 4 inch courses, per square,	1	12	6

Ripping off old shingling, and shingling again with either sort of shingles and courses, charge at the same price as new lathing and shingling; and for lathing only, charge one fourth of the price of the shingling; altering laths or other repairs, charge for by the time spent thereat.

Shingling hips or valleys, at double price.

Valley gutters prepared for lead or copper, per foot, running,	~	~	6

If shingled, add in proportion.

LATHING and shingling penthouses and necessaries, add one half to the price of each sort of shingling before described.

The rafters and joists of penthouses, per square,	12	~

CEILING and end-boards of penthouses, per foot superficial,	~	~	3
Cornice and fascia, per foot, running,	~	1	~

DORMER

L. s. d.

DORMER Windows, flat tops, containing 12 lights (8 by 10 glafs) in a middling pitch, fingle cornice cheeks boarded, each at   -   -   1 10 –

Ditto, with fhingled cheeks, each   -   -   1 17 6

Ridge dormers, with boarded cheeks, each   -   2 10 –

Ditto, double boarded, to appear as fhingling,   2 15 –

Ditto, with fhingled cheeks,   -   ^   3 – –

If the cornice on any of the above defcribed dormers are done any other ways than plain, or the fhingling fhorter courfes than common for three foot fhingles, they muft be valued accordingly.

ARCHED or niche dormer windows, of 3 lights wide, and 3 high to the impoft, with blocks to the fpring of the arch, and a plain fcrowl bracket on each fide, and fhingled cheeks, is worth   -   4 15 –

Ditto, as before defcribed, and 4 lights to the fpring of the arch, at   -   -   -   5 – –

Ditto, with a plain double cornice, pilafters and brackets,   -   -   -   7 10 –

SHINGLING old flat dormers, add the top to the other part of the roof, at the fame price.

Shingling the cheeks of ditto,   -   -   –   10 –

For fhingling the roof of ridge dormers,   -   –   15 –

Roof and cheeks of ditto,   -   -   –   1 5 –

Suppofed to be of middling fize, and three foot fhingles; and if fhort fhingles, in proportion.

Note. Roofs are meafured without any deductions for windows or chimnies.

DOOR

Trap Door & Cheeks from 7/6 to   10 –

If Lined add -   -   -   -   · 3 –

£. s. d.

DOOR cafes plain, with rabbets and bead, per
  foot,   -   -   -   -   -   -   4

Door cafes with fuitable mouldings, ftuff from 5 to
  6 inches fquare, per foot,   -   -   -   6

Ditto, with tranfoms, per foot,   -   -   -   -   -   6½

Door cafes, with mouldings and rabbets, ftuff 6 or 7
  inches, per foot,   -   -   -   -   -   8

Ditto, with tranfoms, per foot,   -   -   -   -   8½

WINDOW frames plain, with proper rabbets, without mouldings or boxings for weights, per foot,   -   -   4½

Ditto, with proper rabbets and boxings for weights,
  without mouldings, per foot,   -   -   -   -   5

Ditto, with mouldings on the face, with boxings for
  weights, per foot,   -   -   -   -   -   5

Window frames, with mouldings and boxed for
  weights, without fhutter rabbets, per foot,   -   -   -   5

Ditto, with proper mouldings, rabbets and boxing for
  weights (ftuff 4½ by 5 inches) per foot,   -   -   -   6

WINDOW frames full trimmed, of the beft kind,
  per foot,   -   -   -   -   -   -   7

CASED frames, when plain, for windows, glafs
  8 or 8½ by 11 inches, made of plank and board,
  with fuitable rabbets, the infide cafings included,
  per foot,   -   -   -   -   -   -   10½

Ditto, with moulding on the front, per foot,   -   -   1   1

Ditto, plain, fuitable for fafhes of glafs 10 by 13 or
  14 inches, infide cafings included, per foot,   -   -   1   4

CASED

	£.	s.	d.

CASED frames, with proper mouldings on the front, per foot, - - - - *1 6*

 If any of the foregoing window frames are made of larger ftuff than is common, add to the price in proportion.

 Note. All door-frames and their tranfoms, and all window-frames, to be meafured the extreme height and breadth at the prices mentioned. The ftuff fuppofed to be of pine.

The arch'd part of common plain frames are worth three times the price of the ftrait part, and thofe with mouldings charge four times the price, when femicircular, and meafured on the extreme of the circular part.

MOULDING fills to windows or doors, fpiked on, or worked out of the folid (if their projeċtions are equal) charge for each, in proportion to the length, from *3/* to - - *3 9*

WINDOW ftools, moulded, rabbeted and properly fixed, are worth for each, - - *6*

CASING door-jambs in frame buildings, rabbeted, meafuring about 20 feet, charge per doorway, - - - - - *3 ~*

Stud cafings for windows of 12 or 16 lights, rabbeted, fit for fafhes, per window, - - *3 ~*

If the fills are made of plank or fcantling, rabbeted for the fhutters, charge each, - - *~ ~ 9*

B   WEA-

	£.	s.	d.
WEATHERBOARDING, rough, per square, - -		4	-
Ditto, jointed only, per square, - - -		5	-
Ditto, grooved or sprung, per square, - -		7	-
Ditto, planed and grooved, or sprung and beaded, the boards of a middling breadth, per square, -		10	-
Ditto, planed, grooved and strait joint, per square,		15	-
ROUGH floors, per square, - - -		4	-
Ditto, jointed, per square, - - -		5	6
Ditto, grooved, per square, - - -		7	-
Ditto, sap'd and grooved, per square, -		11	-
FLOORS of boards, rough edge, *behind Athlins*		5	-
Floors of cedar or pine, not sap'd, planed and grooved, per square, from 11/ to -		13	-
Ditto, sap'd, planed and grooved, from 15/ to		18	-
Ditto, sap'd, planed and grooved, or square edge and strait joint, per square, from 19/ to -	1	1	-
Ditto, with quarter'd stuff, square edge and strait joint, per square, from 24/ to -	1	6	-
All the above floors are supposed of inch stuff.			
FLOORS of 1¼ inch stuff, planed, jointed and nailed through, per square, from 14/ to		17	-
If such boards are grooved, add per square,		2	-
Ditto, with quartered stuff, boards from 6 to 7 inches broad, square edge and strait joint, per square, from 22/ to - -	1	4	-
If such floors are grooved, add per square, from 3/ to - - -		4	-

FLOORS,

	£.	s.	d.

FLOORS, 1¼ inch ſtuff, boards from 3 to 6 inches
broad, ſquare edge and ſtrait joint, per ſquare,
from *24/* to   -   -   *1 10 ~*
   If ſuch boards are grooved, add per ſquare,
   from *5/* to   -   -   -   *6 ~*
   If ſuch floors are nailed in the edge, the head-
     ing joints tongued, add one fourth of the
     prices to each of the above articles; and if
     ſuch floors are dowel'd, add one fourth more.

PARTITIONS of cedar or pine not ſap'd, plan-
   ed one ſide and grooved, per ſquare, from *12/* to   *15*
Ditto, planed both ſides and grooved, per ſquare,
   from *15/* to   -   -   -   *~ 18 ~*
Ditto, of pine boards, planed one ſide, ſap'd and
   grooved, per ſquare,   -   -   -   *~ 17 ~*
Ditto, planed both ſides, ſap'd and grooved, per
   ſquare,   -   -   -   *1 ~ ~*
LEDGED doors, made of cedar or ſap pine boards,
   planed and grooved (hanging and faſtnings included) meaſuring about 20 feet, for each,   -   *~ 6 6*
Ditto, hung with hooks and hinges, well rivetted,   *~ 7 ~*
Ditto, made of pine boards, the ſap taken off, planed,
   grooved and beaded,   -   -   *~ 7 6*
.And when hung with hooks and hinges, rivetted,   -   *~ 8 ~*
    When theſe laſt mentioned doors are batten'd in
    two, four, or ſix pannels, charge for each door,
    from *12/6* to   -   -   *~ 15 6*

               Doors

	£.	s.	d.
Doors made of two thicknesses of pine crossing each other, planed, sap'd and grooved, measuring about 20 feet (hanging and fastnings included) for each door, - - - -		12	—
And when hung double, measuring about 30 feet, charge, for both doors, - -	1	4	—
If doors are larger or smaller than the foregoing, add or diminish, at discretion.			
LEDGE shutters, made of cedar or pine not sap'd, measuring about 10 feet, single hung, with hooks and hinges, each - - -		4	3
Ditto, of pine and sap'd (size as above) hung single, per shutter, - - -		5	—
If batten'd in two pannels, add per shutter,		2	—
Shutters made of two thicknesses crossing each other, of pine, sap'd and grooved, for windows of 12 or 16 lights, glass 10 by 8 inches, hung single, each		8	—
Ditto, double hung, per pair, - -		13	—
Ditto, for 18 or 20 light windows, glass 10 by 8 inches, per pair, - - -		16	—
SHUTTERS framed with a half inch quarter-round, plain raised, two pannels in each shutter for 12 light windows, per superficial foot, - -		1	2
Lining of such shutters, per foot, - -		—	4
Ditto, for 15 light windows, glass 10 by 8 inches, three pannels to each shutter, per foot, -		1	1
Lining to ditto, per foot, - -		—	3½
Ditto, for 18 light windows, three pannels to each shutter, per foot, - - -		1	0½

Lining,

	£.	s.	d.
Lining, per foot, - - -	~	~	3
Ditto, for 24 light windows, three pannels in each, per foot, - - - - ~	~	~	11
Ditto, for 30 light windows, pannels and glafs as before, per foot, - - - -	~	-	10
Lining of fuch fhutters, per fuperficial foot, -	~	~	3

The above prices to include hanging and common faftnings.

If there is a moulding on the pannels, add per foot, - - - ~ ~ 1

If framed with an ogee or ovolo, add per foot, ~ ~ 1

And in proportion for all other mouldings.

Note. All the above fhutters are fuppofed of inch ftuff.

SHUTTERS framed with 1 ¼ inch ftuff, and a 5-8th moulding, the pannels raifed, with a moulding, fizes as before defcribed, add, per foot, to the above-mentioned prices, for framing with the various forts of mouldings, - - ~ 2

Lining at the fame price, if plain.

Shutters for 18 light windows, glafs 10 by 8 inches, bead and flufh on the back fide, per foot, - ~ 1 8

Ditto, for 24 light windows, per foot, - - 1 6

Ditto framed with ftuff 1 ⅜ thick, for 18 light windows, three pannels in each fhutter, bead and flufh on the back fide, per foot, - - ~ - 1 10

If four pannels in each fhutter, add per foot, - ~ 3

Ditto, 24 light windows, three pannels, finifhed as before, per foot, - - - 1 8

If four pannels in each fhutter, add per foot, ~ ~ 2 ½

Ditto,

	£.	s.	d.

Ditto, framed with ftuff $1\frac{3}{4}$ inch thick, finifhed with a three quarter moulding, bead and flufh on the back fide, four pannels in each fhutter, and a moulding on the raifing, per fuperficial foot, — — 2 —

Thofe laft mentioned fhutters are fuppofed to meafure about 20 fuperficial feet.

If the ftiles are rabbeted, and the back pannels nailed, as is fhewn in the plate, charge per foot, — — — — — 2 8

SHUTTERS framed in two parts, and fcrewed together, making about two inches thick, bead and flufh, or pannels raifed with a moulding on both fides, per foot, — — — 2 6

If 4 Pannels add Pr foot — 3

INSIDE fhutters, the back laps framed fquare, to fall behind the wainfcot or architrave, for windows of 18 or 24 lights, glafs $8\frac{1}{4}$ by 12 inches, per fuperficial foot, — — — — 2 —

If the back laps are plain, and only clamped, charge them per foot, — — — 1 3

If divided in four pannels, per foot, — 2 6

Ditto, with mouldings both fides of all the laps, per foot, — — — — — 3 3

SASHES, as common for glafs 10 by 8 inches, per light, — — — — — — 7

The arch'd part of fuch fafhes, per light, — 3 —

Safh-lights in doors, glafs 10 by 8 inches, per light, — 1 —

Ditto, in doors hung in two parts, per light, — 1 2

The arch'd lights, at — — — — 3 —

The wainfcot part of fafh-doors at the fame price as other doors of the fame fort of wainfcot.

Safhes

	£.	s.	d.
Saſhes, 1¼ inch thick, glaſs 9 or 10 by 12 inches, per light, - - - - -		~	10
The arch'd lights, at - - - -	~	3	6
Ditto, 1½ inch thick, the laſt mentioned ſize, per light, - - - -	~	1	~
The arch'd part, per light, - -	~	4	~
Saſhes, 10 or 11 by 13, 14 or 15 inches, and 1½ to 1¾ inch thick, charge from 1/4 to -	~	1	6
The arch'd part from 4/6 to - -	~	5	~
Saſh-lights, 14 by 17 or 18 inches, ſtuff as laſt mentioned, per light, - -	~	1	10

GOTHIC faſhes to any of the aforeſaid ſizes, add one fifth of the aforementioned prices.

	£.	s.	d.
FAN faſhes over doors, as per plate, fig. 1, per light,	~	4	6
Ditto, - - fig. 2, per ditto,	~	5	~
If any of thoſe faſhes are dowel'd, add per light,	~	~	3

MAHOGANY faſhes, to any of the foregoing ſizes, add one third of the aforementioned prices.

Note. All the faſhes muſt be fitted in the frames at the foregoing prices.

	£.	s.	d.
When the meeting rails are thicker than the others, and bevel'd to fit each other, for windows four lights wide, per window, -	~	2	6
And in proportion for larger or ſmaller.			
Window ſtops and grooved laths, per window, *Each*		1	3

SQUARE

£. s. d.

SQUARE show-window sills, worked out of the
  solid, measuring round the returns, per foot, running,   -   -   -   -   — 1 3/6

Plank jambs and head to those windows, per foot,   — — 3/6

Frieze and cornice, if plain, including the astragal
  on the lower edge of the frieze, measuring along
  the upper fillet of the cornice, per foot lineal,   — 2 6

If a fret or dentil, add per foot,   -   -   — — 5

And if the cornice is covered with two inch plank,
  bevel'd, charge per foot,   -   -   — — 8

But if rough, suitable for lead or copper, per foot,   — — 4

SHUTTERS framed, with half inch moulding
  on one side, pannels raised, charge per foot,   -   — 1 4

Bead, and flush on one side, stuff 1⅛ inch thick, hung
  with joint hinges, three pannels in each shutter,
  per foot,   -   -   -   — 1 6

If four pannels in each shutter, per superficial foot,   — 1 9

  If double work, add one third of the above prices.

SASHES, for glass 10 by 12 or 13 inches, per
  light, from // to   -   -   — 1 1

Ditto, for glass 12 by 16 inches, stuff 1¼ inch thick,
  per light,   -   -   -   — 1 6

If dowel'd, add per light,   -   -   -   — — 3

Beading before those sashes, charge per foot,   -   — — 1½

CIRCULAR show-windows, add to the circular
  part one half of the aforesaid prices,   -

If there are open pilasters on each side, proper base
  and caps, charge for each,   -   -   — 12 6

Cornice to such windows, charge the whole in the
  same proportion.

ROUGH

	£.	s.	d.
ROUGH partitions or afhlins, per fquare, -		8	~
Ditto, properly braced with boards, from *8/* to	~	10	~
Studded partitions, per fquare, - / -	~	10	6
Dittto with braces, not framed, but nailed, per fquare,	~	11	6
Rough Board Partition fingil P Square	—	6	
TRUSSED partitions framed, with pofts and braces about 10 or 12 by 4 inches, either ftrap'd to a girder, or with a fill, per fquare, -	*1*	10	~
Ditto, with fmaller fluff than the laft defcribed, from *20/* to - - -	1	10	~
DOOR cafes, made of two inch plank, each	~	5	~
Ditto, with double heads, at - -	~	6	6
Ditto, made of three inch plank, at -	~	6	~
Ditto, with double heads, at - -	~	8	~
If there is a fingle moulding round fuch door-cafes, to receive the plaiftering, charge from *1/6* to	~	2	~
SQUARE wainfcot againft a wall or partition, per yard, - - - - -	~	3	9
Ditto, planed both fides, the pannels raifed on one fide, per yard, - - -	~	4	6
Ditto, raifed on both fides, per yard, -	~	5	~
Wainfcot, framed with a half inch quarter-round againft a wall or partition, pannels raifed or flat, per yard, - - -	~	5	6
Ditto, planed both fides, the pannels raifed on one fide, per yard, - - -	~	7	~

C   Ditto,

	£.	s.	d.
Ditto, framed with the moulding, and raifed both fides, per yard, - - - -		8	3
If the moulding is worked on the pannels, add per yard, for each fide fo done, - -			3
If wainfcot is framed with an ovolo or ogee, add per yard, for each fide fo done, - -			6

WAINSCOT, framed with a five eighth quarter-round againft a wall or partition, the pannels flat or raifed, per yard, - - -   6   2

If a moulding on the pannels, add per yard, -   4

Ditto, planed on both fides, the pannels raifed, and moulding on one fide, per yard, - -   8

Ditto, the moulding framed on both fides, pannels raifed, and moulding on one fide, per yard, -   10

Ditto, the pannels double raifed, and moulding, per yard, - - - - -   12

WAINSCOT, framed with a $\frac{3}{4}$ quarter-round againft a wall or partition, per yard, -   7   6

Ditto, planed on both fides, raifed, and moulding on one fide, per yard, - - - -   8   6

Ditto, framed both fides, the pannels raifed, and a moulding on one fide, per yard, - -   10   8

Ditto, the pannels double raifed, and moulding, per yard, - - . -   14

If framed with an ovolo or ogee, add per yard, -   6

    If any of the aforefaid wainfcot is bead and flufh, charge the fame price as pannels raifed with a moulding.

BISEC-

	£.	s.	d.
BISECTION wainscot, as described in plate, fig. 1, per yard, - - - -		7	6
Ditto, as in plate, fig. 2, per yard, -		10	~
Ditto, - fig. 3, ditto, - -		12	-
PEDESTAL wainscot, add for each yard, more than other wainscot framed with the same moulding, *one - twelfth* - -			
Plain dado wainscot, charge per yard, -		10	~
DOORS framed square, two or four pannels, raised on one side, per yard, - - -		5	~
Two or four pannel doors, framed with a half inch quarter-round, per yard, - -		7	~
Six pannel doors, framed with a half inch quarter-round, pannels raised on one side, per yard, -		7	6
Two or four pannel doors, mouldings on both sides, raised on one side, per yard, - -		7	9
Ditto, double work, per yard, - -		8	6
Six pannel doors, mouldings on both sides, raised on one side, per yard, - -		8	6
Ditto, double work, per yard, - -		9	~
If doors are framed with a half inch ovolo or ogee, add per yard, - - -		~	6
If a moulding on the pannels, for each side so done, add per yard, - - -		~	4
Two or four pannel doors, framed with a five eighth quarter-round, per yard, - -		8	6
Ditto, double framed, and single raised, per yard,		9	6
Ditto, double work, per yard, - -		10	6

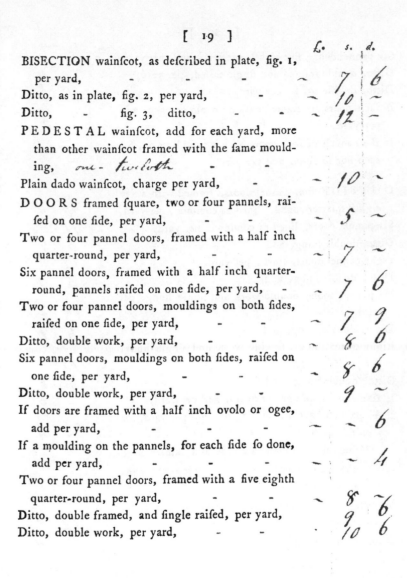

Six

	L.	s.	d.
Six pannel doors, five eighth quarter-round, per yard,	–	8	9
Ditto, double framed and single raised, per yard,	–	10	6
Ditto, double work, per yard, - -	–	11	6
If such doors are framed with an ovolo or ogee, add per yard, - - -	–	–	6
If the pannels of such doors have a moulding on, for each side so done, add per yard, - - -	–	–	4
OUTSIDE four pannel doors, framed with a five eighth quarter-round, lined as common, per yard,	–	10	–
Six pannel doors, lined as common, per yard, -	–	11	–
Ditto, double hung, add - -	–	3	9
Eight pannel doors, lined, per yard, - -	–	12	6
Ditto, double hung, add - - -	–	5	9
Six pannel doors, double work and single hung, per yard, - - - -	–	13	–
Ditto, double hung, add - -	–	6	0
Eight pannel doors, double work and single hung, per yard, - - -	–	15	–
Ditto, double hung, add - -	–	6	6
If framed with an ogee or ovolo, add per yard, -	–	–	6
If the pannels have a moulding on, add per yard, for each side so done, - - -	–	–	4

If any of those doors are bead and flush, charge the same price as ogee or ovolo, and pannels raised, with a moulding on both sides.

Six pannel doors framed with a three quarter quarter-round, lined and single hung, per yard, -	–	12	6
Ditto, double hung, add - - -	–	6	6

Eight

	£.	s.	d.
Eight pannel doors, three quarter quarter-round, lined and fingle hung, per yard, - - -		15	~
Ditto, double hung, add - -	~	7	6
Six pannel doors, near two inches thick, and lined as common, and fingle hung, per yard, -	~	16	~
Ditto, double hung, add . -	~	7	6
Eight pannel doors, two inches thick and lined, fingle hung per yard, - - ~	-	17	6.
Ditto, double hung, add - -	~	7	0
If framed with an ogee or ovolo, add per yard, -	~	~	8
If raifed with a feint hollow, add per yard, -	~	~	10
If fuch doors are lined in the rabbets, add per yard,	~	2	~

If fuch doors are arch'd, or otherwife uncommon, add in proportion to the labour.

	£.	s.	d.
DOOR-WAY jambs of boards in 9 inch walls, fingle rabbet, charge per foot lineal,	~	~	7
Ditto, with 2 inch plank, per foot, - -	~	~	8
Ditto, done with boards in 14 inch walls, per foot,	~	~	9
Ditto, with 2 inch plank in 14 inch walls, per foot,	~	~	10
Door-way jambs, framed with a five eighth quarter-round, three pannels in each jamb, the pannels raifed, with a moulding, per fuperficial foot, -	~	1	2
Ditto, framed with a ¾ quarter-round, per foot, -		1	6
If framed with an ogee or ovolo, or bead and flufh, add per foot, - - -	~	~	1½
If four pannels in each jamb, add per foot, -	~	~	1½

If there are circular fofits, charge them at four times the price of the jambs.

LAD-

	£.	s.	d.
LADDERS, made of poles from 10 to 15 feet long, charge per round, from 9 to -	-	-	10
Ditto, from 15 to 24 feet long, charge per round, from 10 to - - -	-	-	11
Ditto, from 24 to 35 feet long, charge per round, from 11 to - - -	-	1	1
Ditto, from 35 to 45 feet long, charge per round, from 1/1 to - - -	-	1	3
STEP ladders, made of boards, per foot lineal,	-	-	3
Ditto, made of two inch plank, at least two steps let through, per foot lineal, - -	-	-	5
WINDING stairs, not sap'd, from two feet six inches to three feet going, per step, from 1/6 to	-	1	9
Ditto sap'd, size as before, per step, from 2/ to	-	2	6
NEWELS, not sap'd, per superficial foot, from 3 to - - - -	-	-	4
Ditto sap'd, charge from 4 to -	-	-	6
DOG-LEG'D or plain open newel stairs, three feet clear going, the rails kneed and posts cap'd, charge per rise, - - -	-	10	-
For half paces, add - - -	-	15	-
And for quarter paces, charge each at -	-	10	-
If tongued and nailed in the edge, add in proportion.			
Common skirting on the square steps, per foot, -	-	1	-
Ditto on winders, per foot, - -	-	1	6
Ditto on quarter or half paces, per foot, -	-	-	6
SURBASE, like half the hand-rail, per foot, -	-	1	-
Plain pilasters, charge each at - -	-	5	-
Ditto, with proper cap and base, at -	-	7	6

Pilasters

	£	s	d
Pilasters opened, charge each at - -		6	6
Ditto, with proper cap and base, - -		8	-
OPEN newel stairs bracketed, the rail kneed and posts cap'd, three feet clear going, charge per rise,		15	~
Ditto, three feet 6 inches going, per rise, -		16	~
Half or quarter paces, half hand-rail, skirting and pilasters, at the same price as the foregoing stairs; if the rails and half rails are ramp'd, add per rise,		2	6
If such stairs are wainscoted, including skirting, caping and open pilasters, charge per rise, -	1	4	6
For ramps in the wainscot, add per rise, -		2	6
If the wainscot is not pannel'd, deduct per rise, -		1	-
For fluting newel posts, each - -		12	~
And for fluting pilasters, each -		4	~
If the steps and risers are dove-tail'd and glewed together, with the noseings, and bearers at the back, for each step, add - - -		1	~

Note. If such stairs are larger, or any other brackets than plain, they must be valued according to the work.

	£	s	d
OPEN newel stairs, 4 feet between the newel and wall, ramp'd rails and bracketed, the steps and risers dovetail'd and glewed, with skirting, half-rail and pilasters, per rise, - -	1	2	6
If wainscoted, add per rise, - -		12	~
Half paces, dowel'd or nail'd in the edge, -	1	10	~
Quarter paces, each - - -	1	~	~
If the rails are mitred instead of capping, deduct for each post, - - -	~	2	6
A TWIST rail, of one revolution, -	6	~	~

A Twist

	£.	s.	d.
A twift rail, one revolution and a half, -	8	-	-
And for thofe of two revolutions, - -	10	-	-
For fluting newel-pofts, each - -	-	12	-
For fluting pilafters, each - -	-	4	-

> If mahogony is ufed for the pofts, rails, bala-
> fters, pilafters and wainfcot, add one fourth of
> the foregoing prices.
>
> When there is a circular rail to connect any two
> flights together, or when there is more rail
> and balafters at the upper landing than com-
> mon, they muft be valued according to the
> labour.

	£.	s.	d.
TRIANGULAR wainfcot under ftairs, half inch moulding raifed fquare, per yard, - -		10	-
Ditto, 5-8th moulding, pannels raifed with a mould-ing, per yard, - - - -		11	6
LINING of common clofets, preffes or walls, planed and grooved, per fquare, -	-	1	-	-
CEILINGS of houfes or penthoufes, ftrait joint, per fquare, - - -	1	5	-
SHELVES of common clofets or dreffers, per fu-perficial foot, - - -			3
Plank fhelves of dreffers, per foot, -	-	-	6
GLEW'D linings, and fquare fhelves, in the beft fort of clofets, per fuperficial foot, -	-	-	4

	£.	s.	d.

SCOLLOP'D fhelves, the plain fort, per fuperficial foot,   -   -   -   -   -   -   7

Ditto, the neater kind, per foot,   -   -   -   -   8

> *Note.* To meafure fcollop'd fhelves, take eight
> inches on each fide of the door, if the fhelves
> are fo long, or the whole length if fhorter, by
> the full breadth, and the remainder of the
> ends at the fame price as fquare fhelves in the
> fame clofets.

CLOSET fliders clamp'd, each 6/ - to   -   7   6

SHELVES and common counters, in fhops or
ftores, per fuperficial foot, from 2 to   -   -   -   3

Ditto, planed to a thicknefs, with an aftragal on the
edge let into the uprights, per fuperficial foot,   -   -   4

> *Note.* If lefs than a foot in breadth, take them
> lineal at the fame price.

PLAIN jamb cafings of doors or windows, heads
and fills, and other narrow cafings, not exceeding
five inches broad, per foot lineal, from 2 to   -   3

If broader than thofe, add per inch,   -   -   -   -¼

And if a moulding is nailed on, add per foot,   -   -   -   1 ¼

Jamb cafings, not exceeding five inches broad, with
a bead or ovolo worked on, per foot,   -   -   -   -   3 ½

SKIRTING plain, in frame buildings, per foot,
from 2. to   -   -   -   -   -   2 ½

Ditto in brick buildings, of cedar or pine not fap'd,
per foot,   -   -   -   -   -   2 ¼

Ditto fap'd, per foot,   -   -   -   -   3

SKIRTING, with a moulding nailed on, or common furbafe, per foot,   -   -   -   -   6

CASINGS

	£.	s.	d.

CASINGS or rabbets in clofets, &c. per fett, from 1/6 to - - - ~ 2 6

Cafings before fafhes of 12 or 15 lights, glafs 10 by 8 inches, per window, - - - ~ 1 9

Hanging fuch fafhes, per window, - - ~ 1 9

Cafing windows 18 or 24 lights, glafs fize as before, ~ 2 6

Hanging fuch fafhes, - - - ~ 2 ~

> *Note.* The above cafings are fuppofed tongued into the jambs.

BEADING before fafhes, in cafed frames for windows of 18 or 24 lights, glafs 9 by 12 inches, per window, - - - - - ~ 2 6

Hanging fuch fafhes, per window, - - ~ 2 9

> Safhes hung for both to flide, charge at double the aforefaid prices.

Grooved laths and parting ftrips, per window, *Each* 1 3

If the pullies are box'd, per pully, - - - 1 ~

> If windows are larger, or otherwife different, charge in proportion to the work.

Iron Box Nulles pr. Pair ~ - - - 1

FASCIAS, planciers, barge and back boards plain, per foot lineal, - - - ~ ~ 3

BARGE cornices fingle, per fuperficial foot, - ~ 1 ~

EVE cornice plain, of inch ftuff, girting from 20 inches to three foot, per fuperficial foot, - ~ ~ 10

Ditto, 1 ½ or 2 inch ftuff, per foot, - - ~ 1 ~

BLOCK cornice, girting as above, inch ftuff, per foot, - - - - - ~ 1 1

MODILLION cornice, inch ftuff, girting from two to three feet, per foot, - - ~ 1 3

Ditto, made with plank, a feint hollow in the fafcia, per fuperficial foot, - - ~ 1 4

Ditto,

	£.	s.	d.
Ditto, girting about four feet, per superficial foot,	1		3½
If any of the above cornices have a dentle or common fret in the bed-mould, add, for every superficial foot, - - - -			5
If any of the foregoing cornices have coffer'd planciers, for every superficial foot the cornice measures, add - - -			4

> If the plain cornices are raking, add one fourth to the above price of each sort.
>
> And if modillion cornices are raking, add one third more than the level.
>
> To take dimensions of outside cornices, measure on the longest fillet for the length.
>
> *Note.* The covering of return level cornices, at gable ends of houses, to be valued according to the manner of their being done.

	£.	s.	d.
CORNICE and fascia round rooms, per foot lineal, - - - -			7
Ditto, with plain bed-moulds, &c. without mitres, per foot lineal, - - -		1	
Ditto, when mitred, per foot, - -		1	2
Ditto, with dentles or common fret, without mitres, per foot, - - -		1	10
Ditto, mitred, per foot, - -		2	
MODILLION cornices round rooms, with a plain bed-mould, per foot, - -		2	3
Ditto, with a common fret or dentle, per foot, -		2	10

> To measure inside cornices, measure along the wall or wainscot, and at every exterior angle, add two projections to the length.

GROUND

	£.	s.	d.
GROUND frames of boards under architraves, per sett, from *3/* to		4	6
Ditto plank, per sett, from *5/* to		6	6
ARCHITRAVES single faced, five inches and under, on the ground, per foot lineal,		5	
Ditto, exceeding five inches, add per inch,		1	
Architraves double faced, five inches, on the ground, per foot,			6
If knee'd, add for each knee,		1	5½
Circular part of ditto, per foot,		2	
Ditto, fix inches, on the ground, per foot,			7½
If knee'd, add for each,		1	9
Circular part of ditto, per foot,		2	6
Ditto, seven inches, on the ground, per foot,			9
If knee'd, add for each,		2	0½
Circular part of ditto, per foot,		3	
Ditto, eight inches, on the ground, per foot,			10½
If knee'd, add for each,		2	4
Circular part of ditto, per foot,		3	6
Ditto, nine inches, on the ground, per foot,		1	
If knee'd, add for each,		2	7½
Circular part, per foot,		4	
Ditto, ten inches, on the ground, per foot,		1	1½
If knee'd, add for each,		2	11
Circular part, per foot,		4	6
Ditto, eleven inches, on the ground, per foot,		1	3½
If knee'd, add for each,		3	2½
Circular part, per foot,		5	2

Ditto,

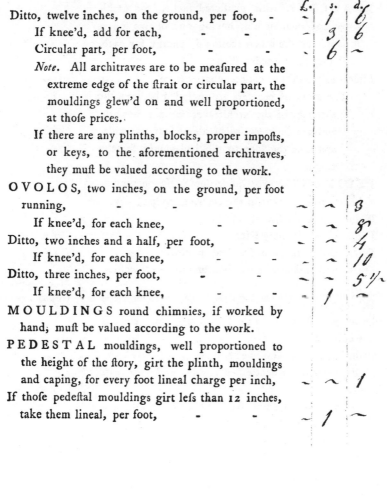

	£.	s.	d.
Ditto, twelve inches, on the ground, per foot, -	—	1	6
If knee'd, add for each, - -	—	3	6
Circular part, per foot, - -	—	6	—

Note. All architraves are to be meafured at the extreme edge of the ftrait or circular part, the mouldings glew'd on and well proportioned, at thofe prices.

If there are any plinths, blocks, proper impofts, or keys, to the aforementioned architraves, they muft be valued according to the work.

	£.	s.	d.
OVOLOS, two inches, on the ground, per foot running, - - -	—	—	3
If knee'd, for each knee, - -	—	—	8
Ditto, two inches and a half, per foot, -	—	—	4
If knee'd, for each knee, - -	—	—	10
Ditto, three inches, per foot, - -	—	—	5½
If knee'd, for each knee, - -	—	1	—

MOULDINGS round chimnies, if worked by hand, muft be valued according to the work.

PEDESTAL mouldings, well proportioned to the height of the ftory, girt the plinth, mouldings and caping, for every foot lineal charge per inch, — — 1

If thofe pedeftal mouldings girt lefs than 12 inches, take them lineal, per foot, - - — 1 —

	£.	s.	d.

B E A U F E T S, with plaiſtered ſhells, the architrave and door arch'd, having one or two ſquare ſhelves, and the others ſcollop'd, charge for each, **5 10 ~**

If they have wooden ſhells, -   - **7 10 ~**

Sliders to beaufets or cloſets, charge from **6/** to **7 6**

The whole of beaufets are included between the extremes of the architraves for the breadth, and are ſuppoſed to be about four feet wide, and from the floor to the bed-mould for the height.

P E D I M E N T S over inſide doors, the opening about 3 feet 2 inches in the clear, as follow, *viz.*

Plain, with a flat frieze, -   - **1 10 ~**

Ditto, with a ſwelling frieze, -   - **1 12 6**

Ditto, with a dentle or fret bed-mould, - **1 17 6**

Ditto, with a dentle or fret bed-mould, and ſwelling frieze, -   -   -   - **2 ~ ~**

Ditto plain, with coffer'd truſſes, -   - **1 17 6**

Ditto, with fret or dentle bed-mould, and coffer'd truſſes, -   -   -   - **2 5 ~**

Plain pediments, with ogee truſſes, -   - **2 2 6**

Ditto, with fret or dentle bed-mould, and ogee truſfes. -   -   -   - **2 10 ~**

Note. The common fret and truſs are ſuppoſed to theſe pediments; if they are different, value according to the work.

If any of theſe pediments are opened on a ſquare, with the rake, add one ſixth of the aforeſaid prices.

	£.	s.	d.

CORNICES level, over infide doors or windows, three feet two inches clear, - - - - — 14 —

Ditto, with a fwelling frieze, - - — 16 6

Ditto, with a coffer'd frieze, - - - — 19 —

Ditto, with ogee or fhaped truffes, and the bed-mould broke over them, - - - 1 2 —

Ditto, with a dentle or fret bed-mould, and flat frieze, - - - - 1 2 —

Ditto, with a fwelling frieze, - - 1 4 6

Ditto, with coffer'd truffes, - - - 1 9 6

Ditto, with ogee or other fhaped truffes, - 1 12 6

Ditto, with a dentle or fret bed-mould, fwelling frieze and cantalivers, - - - 1 17 6

Note. When there are contracted friezes or tablets, or otherwife different from the above defcribed, charge according to the work.

If any of the aforefaid pediments are on the outfide of houfes, and covered with lead or copper, or with boards cut to reprefent fhingling, add for ditto, - - - 10

And if fhingled, or the opening wider than common, charge in proportion to the work.

MANTLE cornices to kitchens, not girting more than 15 inches, per foot, - - — — 10

To meafure them, take the longeft fillet of the cornice for the length, and from the top of the fhelf to the bottom of the rail for the breadth.

MANTLE cornices plain, of a common fize, per foot fuperficial, - - - — 2 —

Ditto,

	£.	s.	d.

Ditto, with common dentle or fret bed-mould, per foot, - - - - - 3 -

If there are fmall fwelling truffes, or truffes prepared for the carver, for each, - - 2 6

And for a tablet, - - - - 1 6

If the bed-mould of the plain mantle is broken, charge for each break, - - - - 8

If the bed-mould and cornice, for each, - 1 6

If the dentle or fret bed-mould is broken, for each, - 1 3

If bed-mould and cornice, for each break, - 2 1

If there is no wainfcot under the cornice, the grounds muft be valued. - - -

If the tablet, truffes or receffes are coffer'd, for each, - 1 6

> Mantle cornices are to be meafured on the upper fillet for the length, and the top with the moulding for the breadth.

TABERNACLE frames on wainfcot, per foot lineal, - - - - 8

Ditto, on walls, - - - - 10

Breaks, charge for each, - - 1 -

> The pannels to be meafured as wainfcot.
> When the mouldings are only nailed on the wainfcot, they muft be valued in proportion to the trouble:

FLAT roofs laid with plank, the bridgings included, per fquare, from 25/ to - 1 10 -

Such roofs laid with two thickneffes of boards, the lower courfe of pine fap'd, grooved and gullied, per fquare, from 30/ to - - 1 16

POSTS

	£.	s.	d.
POSTS and rails framed on flats, the posts prepared for cloath-lines, per foot lineal, - -		1	3
When the moulding of the upper rail is worked out of scantling, or made of plank, with caping and moulding, per foot, - -		1	9
These are supposed to have three rails; and if there are more, add for every additional rail, per foot,			3
BALCONY rails and balusters, about two inches square, per foot lineal, - -		2	
If the rails are ramp'd, add for each, -		5	
Ditto, with balusters 2½ inches square, per foot, -		3	3
If the rails are ramp'd, add for each, -		5	6
Ditto, with three inch balusters, per foot, -		4	
Ditto, with 3½ inch balusters, per foot, -		4	9
If the rails are ramp'd, add for each, -		6	6
Ditto, with balusters four inches square, per foot,		5	6
For ramp'd rails, add for each, - -		7	

If balconies have raking returns, or with red cedar posts, or otherwise different from those above described, they are to be valued according to the work.

	£.	s.	d.
COMMON latticed partitions, planed, per foot, from 6 to - -			8
Ditto in doors, per foot, -			9
LATTICED work, with inch astragal on both sides, per foot, - - -			10
Ditto, in doors, per foot, - - -		1	

E   CHINESE

£. s. d.

CHINESE railing, as per plate, figure 1, of stuff
near 5-8ths by 1 ¼ inches, per superficial foot, - - / 6
Ditto, framed of stuff 1 ¼ by 2 inches, per foot - . 2 -
Ditto, as per plate, figure 2, near 5-8ths by 1 ¼ in-
ches, per foot, - - - . 2 -
Ditto, near 1 ¼ by 2 inches, per foot, - - - 2 6

WAINSCOT in pews, framed with a half inch
quarter-round, and pannels raised square against a
wall, per yard, - - - - 4 -
Such wainscot planed both sides, per yard, - 5 -
Doors in such wainscot, per yard, - - 6 -
If framed with ovolo or ogee, add per yard, - - - 6
Pilasters between doors, where there are single pews,
per foot superficial, - - - / 6
Caping of pews, flat on the top, against a wall, per
foot lineal, - - - - 2½
Ditto, with a moulding on both sides, - - - 4

CELLAR doors ledg'd, about four feet wide, of
pine boards sap'd, and hung double, the cheeks
and fills of pine scantling, from / 8/ to - / - -
Ditto, with red cedar cheeks and fills, from 2 2 to / 4 -
And when hewed out of red cedar posts, from 2 4/ to / 6 -
Such doors, exclusive of their cheeks and fills,
from / 3/ to - - - - 16 -
If such doors are lined, from 3/6 to - - 5 -
If they are hung single, deduct from them - - 3 -
If cellar doors are larger than common, or the
boards quarter'd, or done in a different man-
ner, charge accordingly.

LINTELS

LINTELS over cellar doors, or posts to support the doors when open'd, value them according to the manner of their being done.

PORCHES, with posts of pine or oak scantling, the heads turn'd, from *17/* to - - 18 ~

Ditto, with the posts cap'd, from *20/* to - ~ 1 1

Ditto, with red cedar posts, the heads turn'd, from *21/* to - - - 1 3 ~

Ditto, cap'd, from *24/* to - - 1 5 ~

> Note. Those porches are not to have wooden floors at the foregoing prices; and if done different from those described, value accordingly.

GUTTERS of plank shingled in roofs, per foot lineal, - - - - 1 3

Ditto, preparing for lead or copper, per foot, - - ~ 9

If the lead or copper of gutters are laid by the carpenter, add per foot, - - ~ ~ ~ 6

Common plain gutters under eaves, of scantling from three to four inches thick, and five or six inches broad, exclusive of their putting up, per foot, from *4/* to - - ~ ~ 5

If those gutters have an architrave on them, add - ~ ~ 2

TRUNKS square, as commonly made of boards, exclusive of putting up, per foot, ~ - — — 6

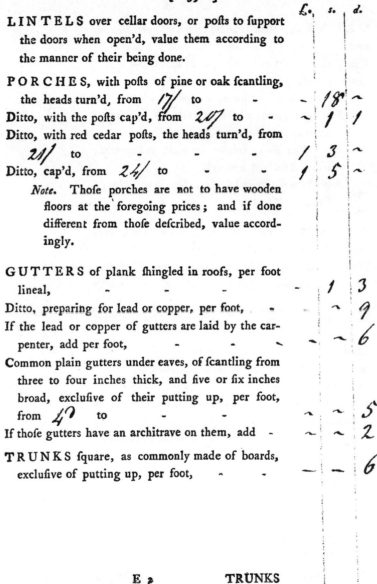

TRUNKS

	£.	s.	d.
T R U N K S, semicircular, made of plank, per foot, - - - -	-	1	-
Ditto, three quarters round, per foot, -	-	1	3
Ditto, round, per foot, - - -	-	1	4
For each break or knee, charge - -	-	2	-
For fixing up any of the aforesaid trunks, charge according to the trouble.			
Note. The above trunks are to be put together with white lead and oyl.			
Any of those trunks having cistern heads, charge from *15* to - -	-	5	-

	£.	s.	d.
C A P I N G of 9 inch walls with fascia, the covering of boards lengthways, per foot, -	-	1	-
Ditto, 14 inch walls, boards lengthways, per foot,	-	1	3
Ditto, 9 inch walls, pitching one way, the boards crosways, per foot, - -	-	1	3
Ditto, 14 inch walls, the boards crosways, pitching one way, per foot, - -	-	1	6
Ditto, pitching both ways, per foot, - -	-	1	9
Ditto, with cornice, fascia and back-boards, pitching one way, per foot, - -	-	1	10
Ditto, pitching both ways, with fascia and cornice on both sides, per foot, - -	-	2	5
Note. The blocks in the walls are included in the above prices.			

	£.	s.	d.
F E N C E S of rough boards, per square,	-	4	-
Ditto, jointed, per square, - -	-	5	-
Ditto, groov'd or sprung, per square, -	-	7	-
Ditto, planed one side, and groov'd or sprung, from *10* to - - -	-	12	-

FENCES

£.   s.   d.

FENCES planed on both fides, and groov'd, per
  fquare, from *14/* to   -   -   -   *17*   *~*
Ditto, ftrait joint, per fquare,   -   -   *1*   *~*   *~*
    If any of thofe fences are batten'd, charge per
      foot lineal for them,   -   -   *~*   *~*   *3*
    If boards are upright, and the tops pointed, add
      to the aforefaid prices one fourth.

CAPING fences, with a moulding on one fide,
  per foot,   -   -   -   -   *~*   *3 1/2*
Ditto, with mouldings on both fides, per foot,   -   *~*   *5*
Ditto, with two or three inch plank, the top bevel'd,
  with pikes put in, per foot, from   *6*   to   -   *~*   *8*
    Note. The dreffing the pofts on one fide is in-
      cluded in the above prices; but if dreffed all
      round, they are to be valued for: Likewife
      the digging of holes.

PALISADE fence, with pointed or round heads,
  in a plain manner, not exceeding four feet high,
  fee figure 1, per foot running, *from -1/6 to*   -   *1*   *8*
GATES, fingle hung, ~~each~~,   -   -   *~*   *9*   *6*
Ditto, double hung, ~~each~~   -   -   *~*   *16*   *~*

PALISADE fence, the heads of the pales and
  pofts cut nearly as figure 2, per foot running,   -   *~*   *2*   *6*
Each ramp,   -   -   -   -   *~*   *4*   *~*
GATES, fingle hung, ~~each~~   -   -   *14*   *~*
Ditto, double hung, ~~each~~   -   -   *1*   *1*   *~*

PALISADE

£.   s.   d.

PALISADE fence, with the pales and posts cut
as in figure 3, the pales sunk even with the rails,
and each rail architrav'd on one side, per foot running, -   -   -   ~ 3   9

Each ramp, -   -   -   -   ~ 8   ~

GATES, single hung, ████ -   -   1   ~   ~

Ditto, double hung, ████ -   -   1   10   ~

    If there is a continued pedestal or plinth under
        any of the foregoing fences, or done any other
        ways not described above, they must be valued
        accordingly.

    The aforesaid fences are supposed from 20 to 40
        feet in length, the posts squared, and the rails
        also prepared nearly the size by the employer,
        at the above prices.

    Note. The digging of the holes for the posts
        are not included in the above prices, that not
        being the carpenter's work.

PALISADE fence, with the pales 1¼ inch square,
the top rail solid, and mouldings each side back'd,
the lower rail of boards or plank, and cap'd with
plank back'd on the top, per foot, from 3/9 to - 4   9

GATES, single hung, each -   -   1   10   ~

Ditto, double hung, ████ -   -   2   5   ~

Each ramp, -   -   -   12   —

CENTERS, that are semicircular, in walls from
    9 to 22 inches, measure the frame and cover, per
    superficial foot, -   -   -   ~   ~   4

Ditto, under common alleys, the frames, per super-
    ficial foot, -   -   -   ~   ~   1½

Covering those centers, per superficial foot, -   ~   ~   1

                            CENTERS

£.   s.   d.

CENTERS under vaults, the frames,

Covering those centers, per square, *from 15/ - to / ~ ~*

GROINE centers, the frame,

Covering those centers, per square, *30/- to - - 2 ~ ~*

CENTERS for stone bridges, not exceeding 20 feet span, the frame,

Covering those centers, per square, *from 15/ - to / ~ ~*

　　If centers are made in any other form, value them according to the work.

RACKS for common stables, the bars planed and properly fixed, per foot running, from *//* to *~ 1 4*

MANGERS, planed on the inside, and properly fixed, per foot running, from *8?* to *~ ~ 9*

RACKS and Mangers for the better kind of stables, planed on both sides, fixed as aforesaid, including the back boards and boards over the rack, per foot, running, -   -   -   *~ 3 6*

STALLS for stables, with a back post planed and a swinging bar rounded, hooped and hung with chains, and an upright board the breadth of the manger between each stall, for each division charge *~ 5 ~*

STALLS, with a close partition, back post and top rail, for each division, charge from *12/* to *~ 15 ~*

GATES, with four bars, and about five feet high and ten feet broad, made of pine, braced and rivetted in every crossing, hung with hooks and hinges, per gate, -   -   -   *1 5 £*

GATES

	L.	*s.*	*d.*

G A T E S, with five bars, from 10 to 12 feet broad, and from five to six feet high, the bars of $1\frac{1}{4}$ inch pine boards, double braced, with two uprights in the middle and rivetted in every crossing, hung as above, per gate, - - - *1 12 —*

Note. The hewing and fixing the posts are not included in the above prices.

C I S T E R N S FOR BREWERIES.

Reservoir, containing near 53 barrels, and 12 to 14 inches deep, per barrel, from *4/6* to - — 5 —

Coolers, &c. of near 45 barrels, and 7 to 9 inches deep, per barrel, from *5/6* to - - — 6 6

Underback, if square, of near 33 barrels, and 4 feet 3 to 4 feet 6 inches deep, per barrel, from *4/* to — 4 6

Working Tuns, if square, of near 35 barrels, and from 4 to 5 feet deep, per barrel, from *4/* to — 4 6

Mash Tub, round, containing near 55 barrels, when about 4 feet deep, per barrel, - — — 4 —

If the Underback or Working Tuns are round, and about the same contents as those that are square, add per barrel, *from 3/6 - to* - — 3 9

If vessels of any of those sizes are oval, add per barrel, *Shillings pr. foot lineal.* - — 3 3

C I S T E R N S FOR SUGAR-HOUSES.

Lime Cistern, if square, and about 7 feet deep, containing near 100 barrels, per barrel, - — 2 —

Mould Cisterns, of 40 barrels, when near four feet deep, per barrel, - - - — 3 9

Clarifying Ditto, of 25 barrels, same depth, per barrel, - - - — 3 9

Clay Ditto, of 35 barrels, same depth, per barrel, — 3 6

Scum

	£.	s.	d.

cum Cifterns, of 5 barrels, when near 4 feet deep,
per barrel,   -   -   -   ~ | 7 | 6

Ditto, of 20 barrels, and near 5 feet 6 inches deep,
per barrel,   -   -   - ‹   ~ | 4 | ~

If cifterns, of fimilar contents and depths, are round,
charge them, per barrel, *1/8 - lefs*

And if fuch cifterns are oval, per barrel, *the Same as Square.*

C I S T E R N S for D I S T I L L E R I E S.

Cifterns, of 20 barrels each, charge per barrel, ⎫ ~ | 3 | ~
Ditto, of 30 barrels each, per barrel,   -   ⎬ ~ | 2 | 9
Ditto, of 40 or 45 barrels each, per barrel,   - ⎭ ~ | 2 | 6
Worm Tubs, containing 20 barrels, per barrel, ⎫ ~ | 3 | 9
   Ditto,   -   40 ditto,   -   ditto, ⎬ ~ | 3 | 6
   Ditto,   -   100 ditto,   -   ditto, ⎪ ~ | 2 | 9
   Ditto,   200 ditto,   -   ditto, ⎭ ~ | 2 | ~

K I R B S of two thickneffes, for the bottoms of wells,
per piece,   -   -   -   ~ | 6 | ~

Ditto, of three thickneffes, rivetted,   -   ~ | 12 | ~

Ditto, for the tops of wells, of 4 inch plank, in-
cluding the windlafs,   -   - | 1 | 15 | ~

H A T T E R S Planks, each   -   - | 1 | 5 | ~

H U R L E S, boards from 3 to 4 inches broad, per
foot,   -   -   -   -   ~ | 1 | ~

L I N T E L S over doors and windows, per foot li-
neal, from *1* to   =   -   ~ | ~ | 2

F   A PUL-

£.　　　*s.*　　　*d.*

A PULPIT, fimilar to that erected in

Ditto, fimilar to that in

Ditto, fimilar to that in

Ditto, fimilar to that in

Ditto, fimilar to that in

> *Note.* The ftairs leading up into thofe pulpits
> are not included in thefe prices.

To measure the ORDERS.

Take the length of the fhaft of pilafters, and of the
die of the pedeftals, between the mouldings, by
the girt.

Take the length of the moft projecting fillet or part
of the mouldings of the bafe or capital for the
length, and girt into the mouldings for the breadth,
and the fame method for the bafe and cornice of
the pedeftal.

Alfo girt the frieze and architrave for the breadth,
by the upper fillet of the architrave for the length.

Girt the cornice, and take the length of the upper
fillet of that member for the dimenfions.

To

To meafure COLUMNS, their BASES, and EN-
TABLATURES, take the fame method.

The PILASTERS and COLUMNS hereafter defcribed are fuppofed at 1 foot diameter or breadth;
if they exceed that fize, or are lefs, charge in proportion.

	£.	s.	d.
TUSCAN pilafters, the fhaft, per foot fuperficial,		1	3
The plinth, bafe and capital, per foot,		3	
The frieze, architrave and cornice, per foot,		1	3
DORIC pilafters, the fhaft, per foot,		1	3
Bafe and capital, per foot,		3	6
Plinth, bafe and cornice of the pedeftal, per foot,		2	
The whole entablature, when plain, per foot		2	4
If the metopes are coffer'd, add per foot,			4
When there are dentils or frets in the bed-mould, add per foot,			3
If there are mutules in the cornice, add per foot,		1	
Where the lozenges (between the mutules) are coffer'd, add per foot,			4
Pilafters to the IONIC order, the fhaft, per foot,		1	3
Plinth and bafe,		3	6
Entablature, where there is a dentil or fret bed-mould (and no modillions) in the cornice, per foot,		2	
When there are modillions, and dentils or frets in the cornice, per foot,		2	10
Glewing up and fquaring to the proper height and projeftion, three quarter capitals, with a mould for the abacus, per piece,	1.	1	6

Die of the Pedeftal to the Doric Nr. p.

	£.	s.	d.
Whole capitals, per piece, - -	1	5	~

The whole of the pedeftal at the fame price as
the Doric.

CORINTHIAN pilafters, charge for the fhaft,

	£.	s.	d.
per foot, - - - -	~	1	3
For the bafe, per foot, - -	~	3	6
For glewing up three quarter capitals, per piece,	1	10	~
Ditto whole capitals per piece, - -	2	~	~
The whole entablature (only dentils or frets) per foot,		2	2

If there are modillions in the cornice, charge per

	£.	s.	d.
foot, - - -	~	3	~

COMPOSITE columns, pilafters, bafes, capitals and entablatures, at the fame price as thofe of
the Corinthian order.

Glewing up columns of plank to any of the orders,

	£.	s.	d.
per foot, - - - -	~	2	9
Bafes to any of the orders, glewed acrofs, prepared for the turner, and fixed up, per foot, -	~	3	6
Alfo capitals for the Tufcan and Doric, per foot,	~	3	6
If bafes or capitals are worked by hand, charge per foot, - - - ,	~	7	6
Fluting pilafters, charge per foot, ~	~	~	9
Ditto columns, per foot, - -	~	1	3

Where columns are turned out of the folid,
charge according to the trouble of procuring
the ftuff, fawing them off, hewing, and at-
tendance on the boring, turning and fixing
them up.

THE END.

THE PLATES

I

End Frame

Shown is the end or gable of a two-story braced-frame
structure, wall openings and studding omitted. Wooden
wall frames are covered in a mere four lines of text, page
3. Philadelphia was a brick-built city; as a fire precaution
no new frame buildings were allowed after 1795. The
price books of New England, where wooden buildings
were common—even in cities—elaborate on carpenters'
details.

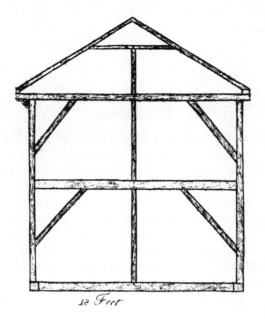

12 Feet

I

Floor Frame

With masonry walls and a 14' front, this is probably intended for a dwelling house. One opening is presumably for a chimney stack and fireplace, the other for a stairway. Joists 9" to 14" deep and spaced 13" to 14" apart are priced (pp. 2, 3) by the square. Extra charge for cutting tenons with "double-tusking"—a refinement that developed strength at the point of bearing. Girders are priced by the running foot with an extra charge for special finishes, such as smoothing by plane or chamfering.

Flooring of various qualities and thicknesses is priced on pages 10 and 11. Boards could be "nailed through" or "nailed in the edge" (elsewhere called "secret nailing"). The doweled type (probably with horizontal dowels, board to board) was the most expensive. It was used in Bishop William White's fine house on Walnut Street the same year this book was published.

III
A Larger Floor Plan

Here we have a brick building two rooms deep with an 18′ front. In Philadelphia this would be characteristically a row building sharing party walls with its neighbors. The two equal openings in the floor are probably for chimney stacks and hearths.

No opening for a stairway is shown. This may well be a ground floor plan, in which case access to the cellar was only by outside bulkhead ladder stairs.

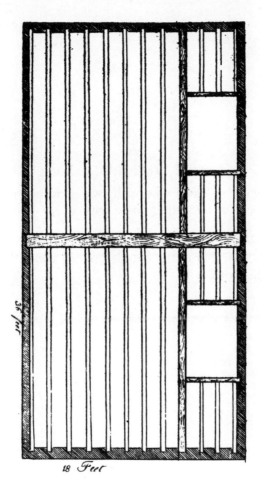

18 Feet

36 Feet

III

Framed Wall with Studding

This two-story end frame with two entrances may well have been for a meeting house with its 30′ gable facing the street.

Here the frame is "full-studded" and ready for nailing weather boarding to the outside (p. 10) and lathing and plastering within.

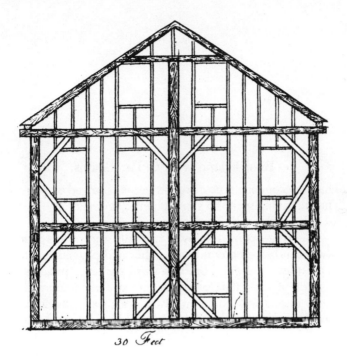

30 Feet

IV

v

Roof Frame with Collar Beams

This very common type of construction is priced on page 4.
The engraving seems to show tapered rafters as sometimes
found in eighteenth-century carpentry.

No ridge pole is shown; typically the rafters would
have been halved around each other and pegged together
at the top. Such long timbers were easier to procure on
this side of the Atlantic where fine, straight lumber from
virgin forests was common. European roof frames were
usually more complicated.

43 Fœt

45'-span Truss Roof

What today would be called a "truss roof" is described (p. 4) as "framed with principal beams, king-posts, braces and purlins," (the last not shown on the plate). Each truss was to be spaced 9' to 10' on centers. Such construction would have been suitable for a good-sized meeting house or a warehouse. The truss is reinforced with iron straps at three points.

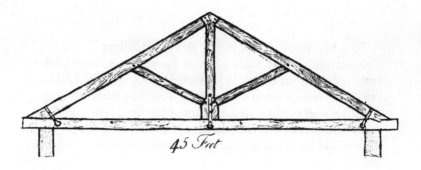

45 Feet

60′ Roof Truss with "Arched Ceiling"

The unusually long truss span of sixty feet is concealed from below by an elliptical plastered vault, thereby avoiding the optical illusion of sagging. The diagonals leading from the wall plates to the bottom of the king post may be what is referred to in the text as a "hammer-beam" (p. 5). This would have made a handsome public room of notable size.

Note increased use of iron strapping.

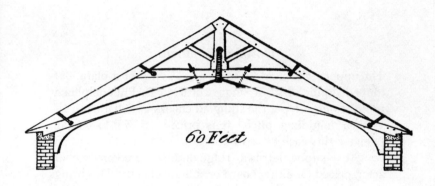

60 Feet

VII

Dormer Windows

The upper right-hand figure is a side view of a plain, flat-topped dormer with a single cornice. In Philadelphia it is of the oldest type; the shingled cheeks are characteristic. With a "middling pitch" it is priced (p. 7) to contain twelve lights each 8" x 10".

At the upper left is a "ridge dormer" of common character, priced for either board or shingle cheeks. This brings the problem of valleys, which could be flashed either with shingles or with sheet lead or copper (p. 6).

The two lower examples are called "arched or niche dormer windows" (p. 7). Decorating the left one are "plain scrowl brackets." The one on the right has pilasters, a double cornice, "gothic sash" and a foliated scroll. Only the greatest houses had such embellishments.

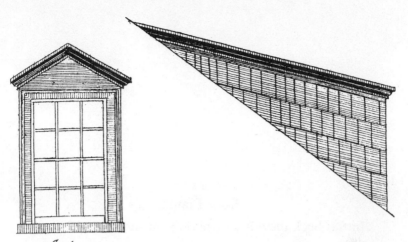

39 Inches

VIII

Door Frames

In this book there is a surprising amount of detail about doors.

Here we have sections of "plank" door jambs and/or heads to be built into masonry walls and strong enough to hold up some of the masonry above.

Each has a rabbet to accommodate a door swinging in, a fore edge trimmed with a bead and in some cases with a backband or brick molding. Classified and priced on p. 8.

x
Window Frames

The two upper figures represent window heads and/or jambs. The two in the center are jambs "boxed for weights" with strips to keep them apart. The sills at the bottom are heavily molded, representing work of unusual quality. Pricing, pages 8, 9.

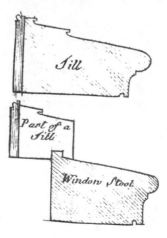

Sill

Part of a Sill

Window Stool

X

Window Shutters

The shutter shown here in full-sized detail corresponds to the description on page 14: 1¾″ thick, bead and flush on the back side, four panels in each shutter and "a moulding on the raising." This is for a large window; the construction is sturdy and the moldings are highly developed.

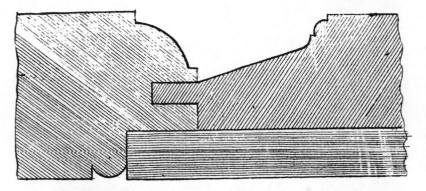

Sash for Doors and Windows

Common, rectangular sash to frame panes 8″ x 10″ were priced at 7 d. per light (p. 14). For an arched top 3 s., or more than five times the former. Prices also varied with the thickness of the sash (1¼″ to 1¾″).

The middle figure shows a door sash "hung in two parts," the mate not shown. This writer can think of no eighteenth-century examples remaining in Philadelphia. They are, of course, typically French.

So-called "Gothic" sash, as illustrated in the fanlight at the bottom, were even more expensive but they were popular, especially for churches and meeting houses, well into the nineteenth century.

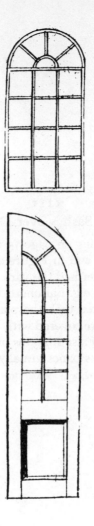

Fan Sashes over Doors

According to the pricing on page 15 the lights in Figure 1 were worth 4/6 each and in Figure 2, 5 s.

Philadelphia never had the variety of fanlight designs found in other places, e.g. Baltimore, but as the years went by metal muntins often took the places of wooden members and the joints were covered with lead rosettes sprigged on and gold-leafed. False muntins of lead or wood strips often divided the glass panes visually.

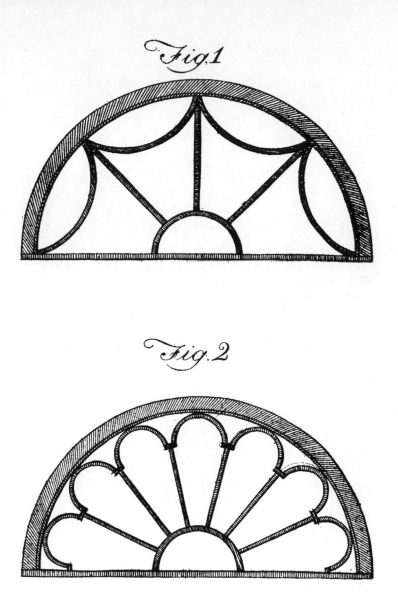

Fig.1

Fig.2

XIII

XIV
Sash Meeting Rails

Full-sized detail of a double-hung window (incidentally, this plate is printed or bound upside down in the original). As described on page 15, the "rails are thicker than others, and bevel'd to fit each other."

The double-hung window—from the standpoint of resisting weather—was such an improvement that it had quickly superceded the casement window from about the year 1700. The cost of hanging such windows is priced on page 26.

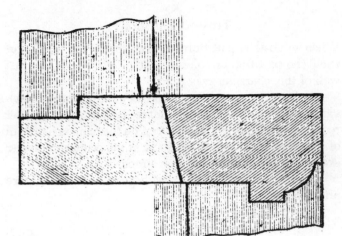

Trussed Partitions

When an upstairs partition between rooms had to support itself (no partition or column on the floor below) a truss wall of this character was used.

It was a common enough problem, as at the Pennsylvania State' House (Independence Hall) where smaller rooms lay above large public rooms on the main floor. Both of the examples shown have doors in the center; the lower example is reinforced with iron straps.

Such partitions "framed, with posts and braces," are priced on page 17.

Paneled Door Details

A considerable amount of variation—and expense—was possible in embellishment by moldings. They are classified and priced on pages 19–21. We have lettered them for convenience.

A. "Framed square," panel raised on one side.
B.   "   "   "   "   " both sides.
C. Framed with quarter round one side, raised panel one side.
D.   "   "   "   " both sides, raised panel one side.
E. A capping piece suitable for church pews, etc.
F. Quarter round on both sides, raised panel both sides.
G. Ogee (reverse curve) one side, raised panel on one side.
H. Ogee both sides, panel has "a moulding on."
I. An unusually elaborate section, decorated on both sides of the door.

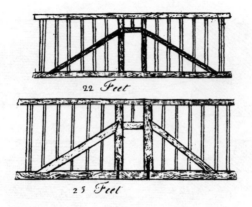

22 Feet

25 Feet

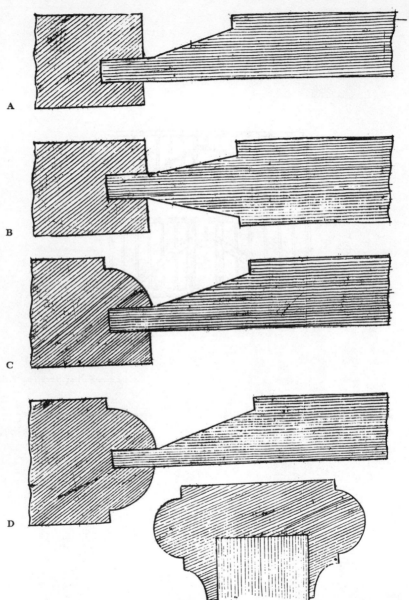

A

B

C

D

E

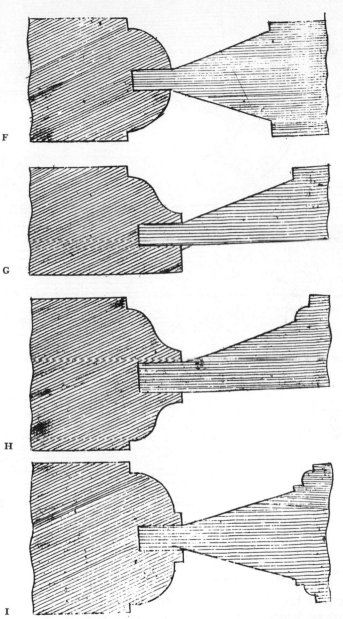

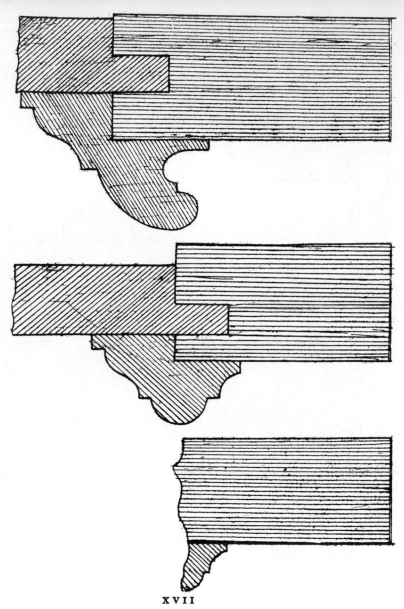

XVII

Bisection (bolection) Wainscot

This type of heavily molded woodwork, more or less an
architectural hangover from the seventeenth century, is
priced on page 19. It is today more often seen in New
England than in Pennsylvania.

Bolection moldings were often used as "surrounds" to
fireplace openings.

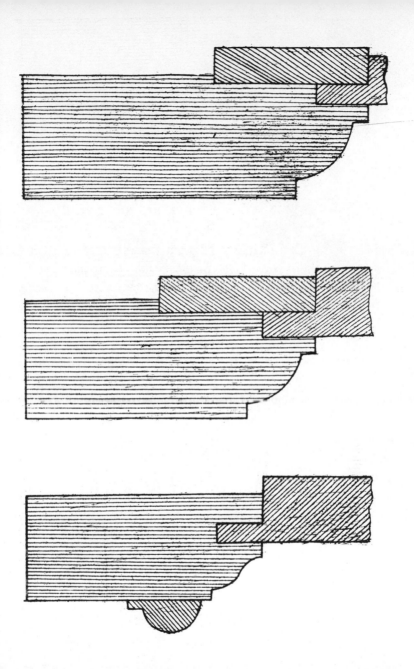

XVII

XVIII
Extra Heavy Paneled Doors

Eight-panel doors two inches thick and elaborately molded like these are priced on page 21. They are the most elaborate the editor has ever seen and were probably intended for public buildings.

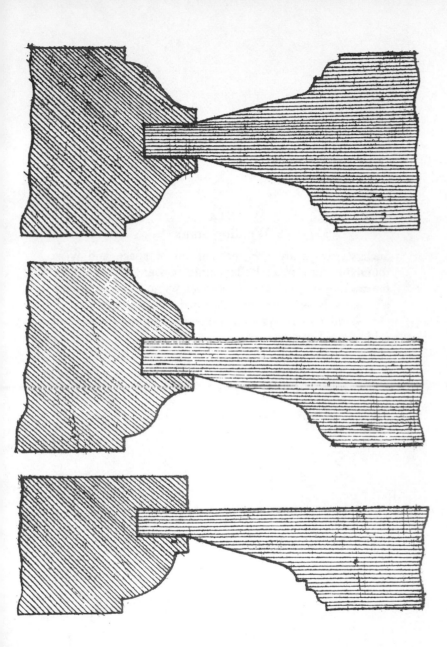

XVIII

XIX
Winding Stairs

Such stairways are very economical of space and were found in many small Philadelphia houses. In the larger houses they often served the kitchen wing. They are priced alternatively as "sap'd" or "not sap'd" on page 22.

Winder stairways are considered dangerous today and seldom used in new work.

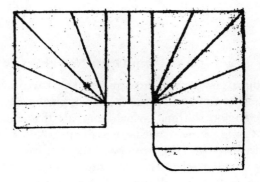

x x
"Dog-leg'd or Plain Open Newel Stairs"

Here the risers turn about—and rest on—a newel post. The straight run of steps at the top is shown finished off with "common skirting" which conceals the ends of the steps. Could be used with—or without—balusters. Cost estimated per rise (riser) on page 22.

For further effect the stair rail could be (and often was) *echoed* in the plaster wall opposite by a half rail ("surbase") and little pilasters answering to the newel posts.

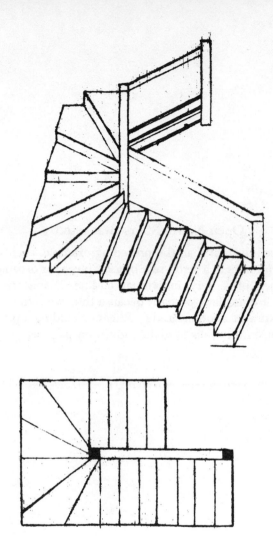

Open Newel Stairs Bracketed

More architectural than the preceding example, each step here terminates in a scroll-saw bracket piece for ornament, sometimes of a very individual outline. Balusters are missing in this plate, perhaps because they were the work of the turner, another trade. Prices, including optional wainscot on the walls to match, given on page 23.

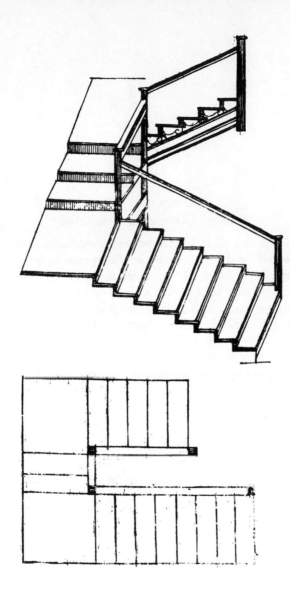

XXI

A Finer Open Newel Stairway

In this example there are further refinements: the handrail is "ramped" and it terminates at the bottom in a "twist of one revolution" over the newel post.

Each four-foot step was valued at 15 s. but for those able to pay more, wainscoting could be added, the newels could be fluted and the brackets carved (pp. 23, 24). Balusters not shown or mentioned.

Prices are quoted for "triangular wainscot under stairs" to fill in the wall space running down to the floor.

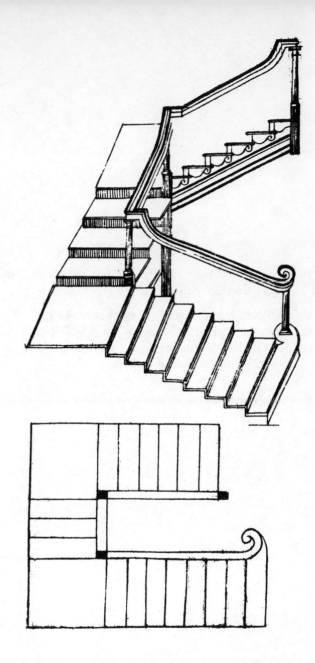

XXII

XXIII
Interior Cornices

The items illustrated here, top to bottom, are priced on page 27 where they are called:

A. "CORNICE and fascia" (a single cornice).

B. "Ditto, with plain bed-moulds" (a double cornice).

C. "MODILLION cornice . . . with a plain bed-mould" (i.e., no dentils or frets).

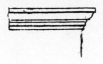

Barges and Exterior Cornices

The two upper figures are of "barges," the narrow boards fastened to the end wall to trim off the crack or joint right under the shingles.

These examples are named and priced on page 26. They are, from top to bottom, identified as:

"FASCIAS, planciers, barge and back boards plain."

"BARGE cornices single."

The three figures below are of cornices which may or may not have contained gutters:

"E[A]VE cornice plain."

"BLOCK cornice."

"MODILLION cornice."

5 d. per foot was asked for adding dentils or frets in the bed-mold. When a modillion cornice was "raking" (run up under the slope of the gable like a barge) one-third was added to the price.

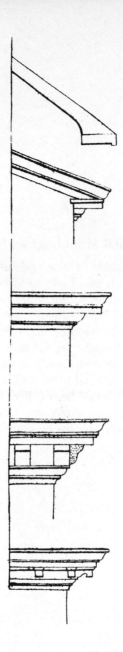

XXIV

XXV
Pedestal Mouldings and Architraves

"Pedestal mouldings" (base and surbase) defining a bold wainscot, plain or panelled, could be found in some of the larger public buildings. They are priced on page 29.

In this period architraves commonly surrounded most openings in walls, exterior and interior. They are designated here as "single faced" and "double faced." Both were trimmed off with beads at the fore edge. Prices on pages 28, 29 include additional charges for curved outlines and for "knees" (elsewhere called dog-ears or crossettes).

The egg-shaped ovolo was a molding less common in 1786, but destined soon to be popular.

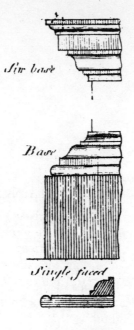

Sur base

Base

Single faced

Ovile

Double faced Architrave

XXVI
Pediments over Inside Doors

(*Left*) Plain pediment with a "swelling" (or pulvinated) frieze (*Right*) Pediment with a broken cornice.

The former is priced on page 30. The latter, often used in cabinet work, is not specifically named here. When used on the exterior the tops of these features were to be flashed with sheet lead or copper—or covered "with boards cut to represent shingling."

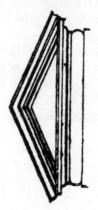

XXVI

XXVII
Georgian-style Chimneypiece in Wood

The text does not describe this attractive design as a composition so the editor will attempt to describe it in the terms of this book—and from other sources.

The chimney opening was probably intended to be rounded by a plaster or marble facing above the plinth blocks at the floor level. Bordering that is a kneed architrave, most likely an ovolo. Immediately above, the frieze is broken by a "swelled truss" at each end and a "tablet" in the center. Above and broken around those three elements is a plain double cornice.

Over the cornice-shelf is a "landscape panel" enframed by a kneed architrave and supported at the sides by carved scrolls. The whole is topped off with a broken pediment.

The chimney breast protruding into the room is trimmed off with a base board, wooden beads for plastering and a plain double cornice at the ceiling. Two chimneypieces of this character were recently added to the fireplaces on the first floor of Carpenters' Hall.

The fancy bolection molding shown in section above is probably to suggest an alternative for the fireplace surround.

XXVII

XXVIII
Chinese Railing

The taste for "Chinese" work made of light sticks was imported from England where it had a considerable vogue. Decoration of this style was not common around Philadelphia.

Hampton Mansion, Baltimore County, Maryland, under construction when this book was published, still has two original Chinese porch railings.

Fig.1.

Fig.2.

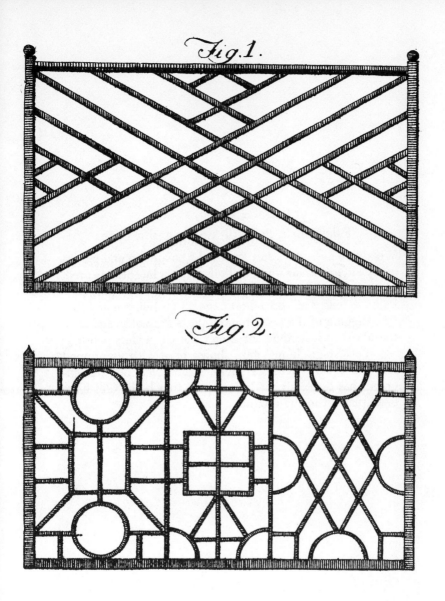

"Pales" for a Palisade Fence and a Gate

Wooden fences and gates are hard to maintain and almost every old one as far south as Philadelphia has disappeared, giving this plate a high value for historical purposes. Palisade fences are priced on page 38 (it being noted that "the digging of the holes for the posts are not included in the above prices, that not being the carpenters' work").

The "single hung" gate shown here with its ramped rail and square pales, or sticks, is notable. But the engraver has carelessly made it appear that both stiles have been planted in the ground.

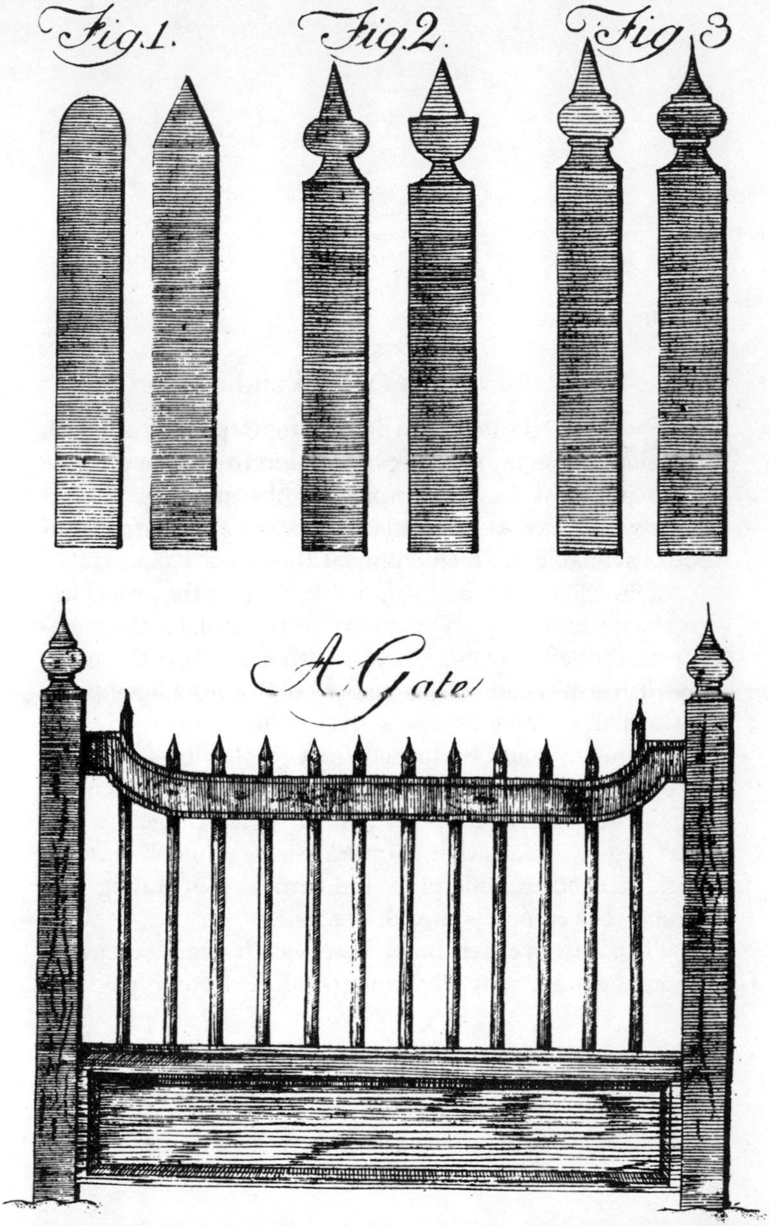

Fig.1.   *Fig.2.*   *Fig. 3*

A Gate

XXIX

The Orders

Four of the classical "Orders" are depicted at small scale in plates xxx, xxxi, xxxii and xxxiii for the purpose of pricing. The "correct" profiles of the moldings of each order would have been available at large size in dozens of books available in Philadelphia at the time.

Directions for measuring work done in the orders are given on pages 42, 43. On each of the four plates the member on the left suggests (being without entasis or taper) that it is a pilaster. The member on the right diminishes upward and evidently represents a column.

Columns could be turned from a solid log (in which case it would have its center bored out to prevent checking) or it could be made of planking glued together and then turned on a lathe. Turning such columns was the work of another tradesman, the turner. But fluting was done by the carpenter at 9 d. per foot.

The Tuscan order shown here was the least expensive; no ornamental extras were suggested. Priced on page 43.

XXX

The Doric

The Doric column as shown here was much like the Tuscan but with a double base. The entablature in this example is ornamented with triglyphs in the frieze and mutules on the soffit or plancher. American carpenters tended to slim down the proportions for wooden construction (especially after the Adamesque proportions came over from England in the 1790's) winking at the laws of the Palladian stone cutters and generally achieving the graceful effects characteristic of the new republic.

Doric parts, with decorative extras, are priced on page 43.

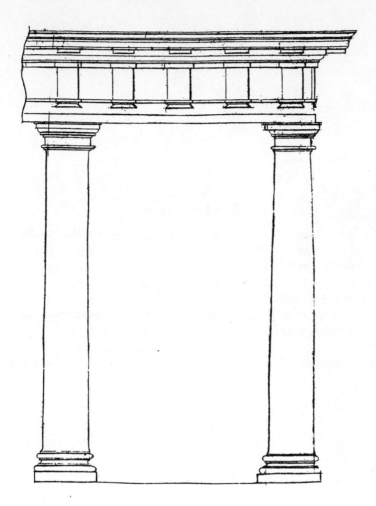

XXXI

XXXII
The Ionic Order

The volutes of the Ionic capital were presumably to be executed by wood carvers who were available in Philadelphia as a ship-building center. In the text (pp. 43, 44) prices are given only for "glewing up" three-quarters and whole capitals.

Dentils, frets and modillions for the entablature were suggested as enrichments at extra cost.

XXXII

XXXIII
The Corinthian Order

The Corinthian order with its foliated capitals was an element requiring high skill in execution. Again, the carving not priced here—only the "glewing up of" three quarters and full capitals (p. 44).

The Composite order is not illustrated in this book but it is priced the same as the Corinthian.

XXXIII

XXXIV
Frontispiece for a Doorway

This example of a doorway flanked with Doric pilasters, capped with a triangular pediment and hung with an eight-panel door seems rather heavy in its proportions and was probably based on some design for execution in stone.

A carpenter doing one of these in wood would probably have lightened its proportions. No specific reference in text.

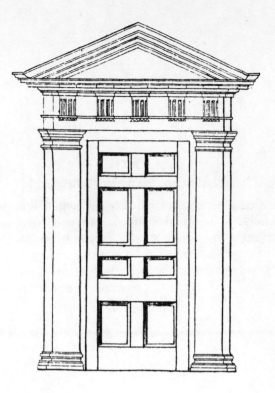

XXXIV

XXXV
Window or Niche Enframement

Raised on a pedestal of window-sill height, this is, architecturally, a highly developed feature seldom seen in American interiors. No specific reference in text.

XXXV

INDEX.

Sleepers

The Carpenters' Company
of the City and County of Philadelphia
1786 Rule Book
Annotated, with an Introduction,
by
Charles E. Peterson, F.A.I.A.